The Skylark Life Skills

Manual

For Women and Girls

Phyllis K. Peterson

Table of Contents

4

Acknowledgements

I wish to acknowledge all of my contacts in foreign countries who have connected me with "Life Skills" educators around the world who have made this book possible. Shiva in China, Naoko Kagami who brought me to Thailand, Irene Taafaki in the Marshall Islands, Johnson Attahbaffour in KwaZulu-Natal South Africa, Mojgan Derekhshani in Johannesburg, Shohreh Azarkadeh in England, and many more. I also wish to thank Kathleen and Kim Babb who have lent me their knowledge of how to create a Kindle E-Book as well as numerous tips on how to create a great book. And a big thank you to my daughter Nancy, photographer par excellence, who designed and created the cover of this manual to suggest transformation and rebirth, budding life, and shadows to depict rage born of oppression.

Preface

Since the summer of 2000 I have traveled the world teaching men, women and children about Protective Behaviors for Children, Boundaries for youth and adults, the Authority of Self, the Importance of the Development of a Feeling Language in Children and Adults, storytelling about the Heroic Female Spirit, Detachment, Anger Alternatives and many other topics. My travel teaching for this cause has been an individual initiative.

I have combined this effort with teaching the Baha'i Faith because all of my work has been inspired by the Revelation of Baha'u'llah.

My heart has been crushed by recent and continuing news accounts of women and girls being assaulted, simply because they want desperately to be educated and to have the Human Rights that belong equally to men and women. This has further inspired me to create a manual of all of my workshops as a Life Skills Educator.

This manual contains knowledge of the history of Human rights from the time of Cyrus the Great of Persia, the battle for human rights during the French Revolution (which disallowed rights for women), plus the ground breaking, monumental work of the

United Nations which has sought to establish equality globally,

The inhumane treatment of women and girls is an affront to every civilized man and woman who values the inborn spirit of those who are innocent, intelligent, indigent or weak. May this manual be a step forward for all who want to assist in ending the nightmare of rape, sexual slavery of children, and the insidious brutality both covert and overt that is committed against women and girls.

A slave today is a man, woman or child who is forced to work and controlled by another person. There are over 12 million slaves around the world (International Labour Organisation) and may be as many as 27 million. Most slaves are in **bonded labour** mainly in Asia or Latin America, this results from a family debt which can't be repaid. In the past slaves were transported across the Atlantic. Today over 2 ½ million slaves are **trafficked** in West Africa, across Europe and between Mexico and the US. There could be up to 8 million children in slavery. Slaves today are worth **less** in real terms than 200 years ago.[1]

---

[1] http://www.betterbytheyear.org/slavery/what_is_slavery.htm

Introduction

By today's standards, something astonishing happened in 539 BCE. Cyrus the Great, a Persian King of antiquity, established the first charter of human rights, which granted rights to slaves to return to their home, freedom of religion, freedom of race, and freedom of language. Cyrus was more than benevolent; he was magnanimous, and his people loved him. His cuneiform cylinder, that outlined his charter, influenced the Greeks and through them, the Romans and the western world. See Appendix I for the translation.

The French Revolution also has its place in the fight for human rights. On August 26th, 1789, the National Constituent Assembly introduced the <u>Declaration of the Rights of Man and of the Citizen</u>[2] (who could only be male), proclaiming liberty, equality, the inviolability of property, and the <u>**right**</u> to resist oppression. These rights are listed in Appendix II. Though this document was history making, it did not address the rights of women and children.

Elizabeth Cady Stanton and Lucretia Mott, however, broke new ground in the framing of injustice toward women as being unnatural and contrary to reason,

---

[2] www.britannica.com

during the Seneca Falls Convention of women's rights in July of 1848. Stanton's cogent Declaration of Sentiments, a virtual replica of the Declaration of Independence, is also listed in Appendix III.

The next major accomplishment came on December 10th, 1948 with the Universal Declaration of Human Rights, which was adopted by the UN General Assembly. You can read through your rights in Appendix IV.

Then, the Declaration of the Rights of the Child was delineated in 1959[3] (You'll find them in Appendix V); and finally, the UN has seen the need to declare the first International Day of the Girl child on October 11th, 2012. This year's theme is connected to banning the marriage of the girl child under the age of 18 so that she can be educated to be physically and psychologically fit for adulthood.

International Day of the Girl Child is an international observance day declared by the United Nations. October 11, 2012, was the first Day of the Girl. The observation supports more opportunity for girls, and increases awareness of inequality faced by girls worldwide based upon their gender. This inequality includes areas such as access to education, nutrition, legal rights, medical care, and protection

---

[3] Adopted by UN General Assembly Resolution 1386 (XIV) of 10 December

from discrimination, violence and unfree child marriage,[4] which is a fundamental human rights violation and impacts all aspects of a girl's life. Child marriage denies a girl of her childhood, disrupts her education, limits her opportunities, increases her risk to be a victim of violence and abuse, jeopardizes her health and therefore constitutes an obstacle to the achievement of nearly every Millennium Development Goal (MDG) and the development of healthy communities.[5]

This focus on human rights for women and girls has a direct tie to the concept of "the authority of self," which I define in my book, "Assisting the Traumatized Soul," as the freedom and ability to use birth-right mental and spiritual powers to make rational and moral choices, self-regulation of the emotions; and the right or permission to act independently with the understanding that one has personal limitations.[6] Without the authority of self women and girls cannot negotiate their way in their families or the outside world.

'Abdu'l-Baha, the Son of Baha'u'llah, the newest Manifestation from God, says that mankind is in need of new powers and virtues, new moralities, new capacities in the day in which we live.[7] They are fully

---

[4] http://en.wikipedia.org/wiki/International_Day_of_the_Girl_Child
[5] http://www.un.org/en/events/girlchild/
[6] Phyllis Peterson, "Assisting the Traumatized Soul," copyright 1999, Baha'i Publishing Trust, Wilmette
[7] 'Abdu'l-Baha in London, page 1

within our grasp....such as the power of speech, the power of choice, the power of discernment, the power of reasoning, the power of identity, the power of wisdom, the power of faith, the power of intuition, the power of reflection, discovery, and understanding....the power of will, memory and the independent search for truth....the power of response, anticipation, attention, and receptivity.... the power of reasoning and deduction, the power of acknowledgement, the power of reciprocity, the power of accountability...and the power of conscience. I have defined each of these powers psychologically and theologically in my book, "Assisting the Traumatized Soul". They are also defined in this book in Chapter Three in the story "The Chalice of Power."

Essentially both women and children have all of these powers. We use them only with differing degrees of proficiency and if we live in an egalitarian or democratic system. Parents grant them incrementally to children as they show responsibility and cooperation. If we have rights, we are allowed to use our powers to the fullest extent, again with the understanding that we have personal limitations and spiritual responsibilities.

"They whom God hath endued with insight will readily recognize that the precepts laid down by God constitute the highest means for the maintenance of order in the world and the security of its peoples."[8] So here we have the balance. We are granted power by God in His Sacred Texts, but His commandments trump the standards of a world careening out of control. We have to be educated in how to use our powers and see their "spiritual essence", especially if we have never been allowed the freedom to use them.

Woman can be forced to exist in a stultifying culture or she can step out into a new paradigm that grants her the right to use the authority of self to change her circumstances for the better. Those cultures that would deny woman her human right to use her power of volition and will have to trust that woman has a conscience and that the Baha'i woman will perceive right and wrong through an in-depth independent search of truth and from the Divine Teachings of Baha'u'llah. In the following quotation from the Universal House of Justice it says:

> "This brings us to the specific points raised in your email of ... As you well understand, not only the right but also the responsibility of each believer to explore truth for himself or herself are fundamental to the Bahá'í teachings. This principle is an integral feature of the coming of age of humankind, inseparable from the social transformation to which Bahá'u'lláh is calling the

---

[8] Baha'u'llah, The Kitab-I-Aqdas: The Most Holy Book, Baha'i World Center, Universal House of Jusrtice, © 1992, p. 21-22

peoples of the world. It is as relevant to specifically scholarly activity as it is to the rest of spiritual and intellectual life. Every human being is ultimately responsible to God for the use which he or she makes of these possibilities; conscience is never to be coerced, whether by other individuals or institutions.

Conscience, however, is not an unchangeable absolute. One dictionary definition, although not covering all the usages of the term, presents the common understanding of the word "conscience" as "the sense of right and wrong as regards things for which one is responsible; the faculty or principle which pronounces upon the moral quality of one's actions or motives, approving the right and condemning the wrong".

The functioning of one's conscience, then, depends upon one's understanding of right and wrong; the conscience of one person may be established upon a disinterested striving after truth and justice, while that of another may rest on an unthinking predisposition to act in accordance with that pattern of standards, principles and prohibitions which is a product of his social environment. Conscience, therefore, can serve either as a bulwark of an upright character or can represent an accumulation of prejudices learned from one's forebears or absorbed from a limited social code."[9]

From this quotation we can discern that the conscience of the individual can be based on the social reality that we live in, which includes such things as prejudice, fantasy, superstition, and false political, national, or religious ideology; or it can be based on divine Revelation.

While I call this a "life skills manual for women and girls" it serves many purposes, such as being a "parenting manual" for men and women, as well as offering a gentle awakening for men of the hidden ways women are oppressed by the ancient traditions of our cultures.

Chapter One will outline the Covenant of God in the Baha'i Faith through which we come to further understand our limits in comparison to the vast amount of human rights and powers God has bestowed upon us.

---

[9] The Universal House of Justice, 1998 February 8, Issues Related to Study Compilation

Chapter One

The Appointment of Authority

By the Covenant of God

"And it is a basic principle of the Law of God that in every Prophetic Mission, He entereth into a Covenant with all believers--a Covenant that endureth until the end of that Mission, until the promised day when the Personage stipulated at the outset of the Mission is made manifest."[10]
'Abdu'l-Bahá, SWAB, p. 207

"A Covenant in a religious sense is a binding agreement between God and man, whereby God requires of man certain behavior in return for which He guarantees certain blessings, or whereby He gives man certain bounties in return for which He takes from those who

---

[10] 'Abdu'l-Bahá, Selections From the Writings of Abdu'l-Baha, Baha'i World Center, © 1978, p. 207

accept them an undertaking to behave in a certain way."[11]

I write this chapter as your sister and your friend. I write it wishing to share with you what I have learned about authority. I claim no power, nor do I want power over anyone. I simply want others to know the peace and order I have discovered first through relinquishing my inordinate fear of authority and then through recognizing that I have boundaries beyond which I cannot go without disobeying God.

Whether you have suffered at the hands of an oppressor, are grappling as a youth with the concept of authority and are reluctant to fully embrace it, or have long ago dismissed authority as irrelevant to your pursuit of individuality, know that distrust of authority is a worldwide phenomenon. Not a day goes by that the headlines of the news organizations aren't blazoned with corporate crime, child abuse by those in position of leadership/authority, ethnic cleansing, and terrorism based solely on religious teachings that have been perverted.

Bahá'u'lláh , the Founder of the Baha'i Faith and His son 'Abdu'l-Baha, suffered terrible hardships for the

---

[11] Universal House of Justice, Compilation of Compilations, Vol. 1, p. 111

purpose of bringing humankind to unity, concord, cooperation, justice, forbearance, fellowship, chastity, illumination, transformation, regeneration, tranquility and peace. This will require that all of mankind turn in trust to a single point of absolute truth, the universal perception of the Prophet, based on the oneness of humankind. With this new perception acquired knowledge from a social reality that is defective will be shed or confirmed, the contradictions that have become as veils for the various types of minds will disappear into oneness and humankind will attain its highest potentiality.[12]

The 50 years plus of imprisonment Bahá'u'lláh and ''Abdu'l-Bahá endured is symbolic of the imprisonment of all of us whether we live in a concrete prison or the prison of self. The oppression They experienced is symbolic of the fact that none of us escapes oppression. We have friends and relatives who are homeless or are counted with those who suffer from mental illness, and we suffer with them. We know brothers and sisters who have acquired the AIDs virus. Joblessness and economic inequality are worldwide touching all cultures and causing increasing stress and distressing migration. The lifetime sacrifice of our Forerunner is an example of the higher pathway we, too, can choose when we are contemplating acts and deeds of unity or hardening our hearts with contention when under stress.

---

[12] See Selections from the Writings of 'Abdu'-Baha, p. 63)

We have yet to discover the spiritual brotherhood that can help us transcend the stresses of our times. But what is to motivate us towards unity? Surprisingly enough it is simply the act of obedience to authority, an act the majority of us fear because we have seen and experienced tyranny and injustice at the hands of authority. We have become jaded in a world where one after another our political, corporate and religious leaders have failed us whether by ignorance, lust, greed or want for power. Yet something within us continues to long for justice, a longing that can only be satisfied by an authority that nurtures us through the many illnesses that mankind suffers in this present day.

Bahá'u'lláh brings us to the heart of the issue with this quotation:

> "And further We have said: "That which God hath ordained as the sovereign remedy and mightiest instrument for the healing of the world is the union of all its peoples in one universal Cause, one common Faith. This can in no wise be achieved except through the power of a skilled, an all-powerful, and inspired Physician."[13]

We know that the entire world is in dire need of regeneration. Witness the percentages of peoples

---

[13] Bahá'u'lláh, Epistle to the Son of the Wolf, Baha'i Publishing Trust, Wilmette, IL, © 1988, p. 62

who are addicted to alcohol, drugs, and sex, together with homelessness that is born of materialism and corruption. This is a world that is indeed being torn apart because it lacks a structure that includes limits. What it needs is a unifying force that will shore up morality, a force that will show us the purpose and benefit of authority that seeks the common good. That force is the Covenant of God. The Covenant is the axis, the pivot upon which all the ills of mankind will be resolved. It includes the promise that God would send a succession of Messengers to meet the needs of an ever-advancing civilization, the needs that humanity faces in the present moment.

"Contemplate with thine inward eye the chain of successive Revelations that hath linked the Manifestation of Adam with that of the Báb. I testify before God that each one of these Manifestations hath been sent down through the operation of the Divine Will and Purpose, that each hath been the bearer of a specific Message, that each hath been entrusted with a divinely-revealed Book and been commissioned to unravel the mysteries of a mighty Tablet. The measure of the Revelation with which every one of them hath been identified had been definitely fore-ordained. This, verily, is a token of Our favor unto them, if ye be of those that comprehend this truth...." (Bahá'u'lláh, Gleanings from the Writings of Baha'u'llah, p. 74-75)

This is but a sample of the divine unity that exists between all of the revelations that God has sent down.

If we agree that there is only one God, then it follows that He has sent all of the religions, all of the Prophets and all of the Holy Books for the purpose of building His Kingdom on earth.

And while each Manifestation was fore-ordained to unravel the mysteries and was a carrier of a specific message, the world was not ready for massive unification and large scale wondrous advancement as it is now. This precious Covenant requires protection in the era in which we live because the potential of mankind is so very great compared to other dispensations. There has to be a system whereby several things have to fall into place in order to preserve unity. The Covenant of Bahá'u'lláh, His Will and Testament, is the distinguishing feature of His Revelation, setting it apart from others. It answers with grand Design the following questions. Who takes over the leadership role when the Manifestation ascends from this world? How is His will to be carried out so that His plan does not fail as happened in the case of Muhammad who left only verbal instructions when He ascended?

Therefore, another facet of the Covenant consists of the Messenger passing on "authority" to an appointed successor as Bahá'u'lláh designated His son, 'Abdu'l-Bahá to be His successor. This appointment was important for the protection of the Cause of God and Bahá'u'lláh gave specific instructions in writing that would leave no lover of the Cause confused.

"Whoso turneth towards Him ['Abdu'l-Baha] hath turned towards God, and whoso turneth away from Him hath turned away from My beauty, hath repudiated My Proof, and transgressed against Me. He is the Trust of God amongst you, His charge within you, His manifestation unto you and His appearance among His favored servants... We have sent Him down in the form of a human temple. Blest and sanctified be God Who createth whatsoever He willeth through His inviolable, His infallible decree. They who deprive themselves of the shadow of the Branch, are lost in the wilderness of error, are consumed by the heat of worldly desires, and are of those who will assuredly perish." (Bahá'u'lláh, Shoghi Effendi, The World Order of Baha'u'llah, p. 135)

"Abdu'l-Bahá is a name that translates into "Servant of God", thus He becomes the person we are to emulate; a Master of all of the teachings of Bahá'u'lláh, and the person who became the source of "Authority" in His absence.

Embedded in the Writings of Bahá'u'lláh, is a further appointment of a Guardian of the Cause of God upon "Abdu'l-Bahá's passing. This Guardian, Shoghi Effendi, "Abdu'l-Bahá's grandson, would go on to develop the Administrative order of the Baha'i Faith, as well as interpret the Writings, translate major texts upon the passing of "Abdu'l-Bahá, thus continuing to protect the Faith from schism.

And finally, the 9 members of the Universal House of Justice, located at the World Center in Haifa, Israel, elected every 5 years, are guiding 7 million Bahá'is who live in all the countries of the world. "Although not invested with the function of interpretation, the House of Justice is in a position to do everything necessary to establish the World Order of Bahá'u'lláh on this earth."[14]

This is the structure, the structure of divine authority, upon which order will be created in this world. The Message of Baha'u'llah will regenerate all the systems of government, education, science, philosophy, and judiciary. Not only will these systems promote justice, but they will also protect the spiritual brotherhood that is vital to maintaining the equilibrium of this world. Conscious knowledge of that spiritual brotherhood can guide us as individuals or systems to the place where each brother holds the other as higher than himself, a form of the Golden Rule found in all of the religions.[15] And just as important, each individual will cooperatively seek the common good.

---

[14] Universal House of Justice, Wellsprings of Guidance, 9 March 1965, p. 52-53
[15] Chapter 5 will examine how the spiritual brotherhood of mankind is protected by the development of virtues.

It becomes necessary also to define *just* authority, so that all may recognize where to turn in trust and become confident that such trust is justified. A rational, nurturing, and *just* authority treats all as equal with the right to dignity even though they may not have the same power, intellectual capacity, experience or material status. A just authority based upon the Revelation of God and submission to His Covenant helps those under its care discover who they are through steadfast love, tolerance, and non-controlling encouragement.

Another aspect of just authority is that it recognizes that this is a new day in which we live, a day in which the individual is granted greater power than past centuries as this quotation from "Abdu'l-Bahá reveals:

"This is a new cycle of human power. All the horizons of the world are luminous, and the world will become indeed as a garden and a paradise. It is the hour of unity of the sons of men and of the drawing together of all races and all classes. You are loosed from ancient superstitions which have kept men ignorant, destroying the foundation of true humanity."[16]

How will we use our power? What constitutes the power of the individual? What powers can loose us from ancient superstitions, traditions and ignorance?

---

[16] 'Abdu'-Baha, 'Abdu'l-Bahá in London, p. 19

In my first book, "Assisting the Traumatized Soul," I showed how I was rendered powerless as a child, and then led step by step to an understanding of how to tap those gems within, placed there by a loving Creator.

Our Creator would not grant power to us unless He also set limits and boundaries for those powers. If we go beyond those limits we will not only lose our psychological balance, but our spiritual balance. We will suffer a loss of tranquility.

In essence, the laws of God are the boundaries or limits that He sets for us. The following statute states His will with clarity:

> "O OPPRESSORS ON EARTH!
> Withdraw your hands from tyranny, for I have pledged Myself not to forgive any man's injustice. This is My Covenant which I have irrevocably decreed in the preserved tablet and sealed with My seal."[17]

This commandment goes out not only to dictators, terrorists and those who participate in ethnic cleansing, but to those who are involved in corporate crime; those who commit child abuse, batter women or men; those who deal in drugs and even those who mistreat prisoners, as well as the

---

[17] Baha'u'llah, Persian Hidden Words #64, Australia, © 1995

prisoners themselves. There are many forms of tyranny.

There was a youth in my community who had read the above quotation of Bahá'u'lláh and said that it portrayed a wrathful God to him. I asked him if he had ever beaten a woman or killed anyone or stolen something. He replied, "Of course not!" Then I told him, "Don't you think it would be important that God make some provision for such things in His newest revelation in order that women and children would be protected? As important and far reaching as the 10 commandments are, there is no commandment that says, "Thou shalt not beat your wife and children." There were even laws on the books in Great Britain that allowed for such beatings at the time Bahá'u'lláh wrote this commandment if you used the appropriate size stick for it."

A letter written on behalf of the Universal House of Justice states,

> "The use of force by the physically strong against the weak, as a means of imposing one's will and fulfilling one's desires, is a flagrant transgression of the Bahá'í Teachings. There can be no justification for anyone compelling another, through the use

of force or the threat of violence, to do that to which the other person is not inclined."[18]

Thus the hand of the violator is stayed by the protecting, uncompromising, and vigilant influence of the institutions of the Baha'i Faith, a fulfillment of the Covenant.

However, Bahá'u'lláh also writes encouragingly to those who repent and acquiesce to living within the boundaries God has set for them.

"Wherefore, hearken ye unto My speech, and return ye to God and repent, that He, through His grace, may have mercy upon you, may wash away your sins, and forgive your trespasses. The greatness of His mercy surpasseth the fury of His wrath, and His grace encompasseth all who have been called into being and been clothed with the robe of life, be they of the past or of the future. (The Summons of the Lord of Hosts, p. 207-208.)

He even indicates that the Word of God has "...established the ignorant upon the seats of learning, and elevated the oppressor to the throne of justice."[19]

---

[18] Violence and the Sexual Abuse of Women and Children, A Letter Written on Behalf of the Universal House of Justice to an Individual Believer, 24 January 1993. Baha'i World Center, Haifa, Israel
[19] Bahá'u'llah, Kitab-i-Iqan, Baha'i Publishing Trust, Wilmette, IL © 1950 p. 60

A sincere change of life is the deciding factor in embracing individuals who have transgressed in the past, says Shoghi Effendi, "The Guardian does not feel that, if a person has approached this Cause and desires to become a Bahá'í, and is determined to change his way of life, his past should be held against him. Where would forgiveness be if every prospective Bahá'í was judged by his past! But once a Bahá'í, a change of life is expected and hoped for, and the friend must help the people to change."[20]

Baha'u'llah also speaks of the attitude with which we must obey His commandments,

"O SON OF BEING! Walk in My statutes for love of Me and deny thyself that which thou desirest if thou seekest My pleasure."[21]

This implies that He would rather we obey Him out of love than fear, though fear is a powerful and important motivator for change.

There is no way we can carry on our life without knowing what appropriate limits and boundaries are. Oddly enough we discover this through our own "authority" or power.

---

[20] From a letter written on behalf of Shoghi Effendi to an individual believer, June 29th, 1951
[21] Baha'u'llah, Arabic Hidden Words #38, Australia

Ian Semple, a member of the Universal House of Justice, has explored the concept of the power of self, or "the authority of self" in the light of five processes. The first is to accept personal responsibility and accept one's self as the ultimate source of authority; the second is to recognize personal fallibility; the third is to recognize a source of authority outside oneself; the fourth is to understand the requirements of the authority thus recognized; and the fifth is the exercise of judgment in carrying out these requirements.

"The first is to accept oneself as the ultimate source of authority. The foundation for all development is to know oneself and to accept one's own responsibility for one's own life.

In . . . a multitude of . . . passages, Bahá'u'lláh's first call to us is not to obey, but to use our minds, to judge fairly, to recognize, and then to believe and then to obey. He assures us that we have the capacity to recognize the truth and to follow it. That ultimate authority resides in ourselves is true for any human being, whether he understands it or not.

The second process is to recognize one's own insufficiency, learning that for a person to follow his own inclinations in everything leads to chaos in his own life and in society as a whole.

The third is to validate a source of authority outside oneself. This leads one to search for an external source of authority, for what is truth. When one thinks one has found such a source it is essential to validate it. To fail to do so is to sacrifice one of the most fundamental rights and duties of a human being.

The fourth is the process of understanding the requirements of that source of authority. Having decided that a source of authority is valid, and that one wishes to obey it, one can only put this into practice if one understands what that source of authority requires.

And the fifth is the role of judgment in carrying out these requirements. Unless one uses one's intelligence and good judgment in exercising obedience to authority, one may well end up doing the opposite of what it really intends.

All five of these processes require the exercise of one's reasoning powers. They are the negation of the concept of "blind obedience," and I believe that this concept of blind obedience is contrary to the spirit of the faith. Obedience for a Bahá'í, is the free exercise of one's will to follow what one believes to be right. Blind obedience is the abdication of one's free will."[22]

---

[22] Ian Semple,From an address titled "Obedience" presented in connection with the "Spiritual Enrichment Program" at the Baha'i World Center, July 26, 1991, Available in "Assisting the Traumatized Soul" by Phyllis Peterson, p.157.

Blind obedience to authority is the abdication of one's authority of self, without choice, upon the explicit commands of an external source. This differs from genuflection in which the authority of self and all of its accompanying powers are, by choice and discernment, willingly offered up out of love in obedience to the commandments of God. Many people who have been traumatized have experienced an excess of authority and would rightly be fearful of blind obedience, having developed a passive response to life. But knowing we are fallible, we can acknowledge our need to turn towards a higher source of truth that will enable us to attain our highest possibilities. We can develop full-hearted obedience to laws we cannot understand but know must be right.[23] Yes, it's a leap of faith, but a faith based on discernment! And by accepting the limits and boundaries set for us by this highest truth, we can disentangle ourselves from the conflicting demands of this shattered and confused world we are living in.

Overcoming Fear of Authority

A prevailing fear of authority is often the result of trauma and sexual abuse. My journey has included the healing of this fear. It has not been a straight path. It has been fogged by paranoia. And it has required a trust in Bahá'u'lláh that has helped me differentiate true thoughts from those that would set my heart racing with adrenalin.

The healing began with a mystical experience that I had in July of 2000. I was walking in the Mall and all of a sudden there was a tremendous "power" that gripped me, similar I think to Jacob wrestling with the angel. That's the only experience to which I can relate it. This power, non-stop for about 25 to 30 minutes, kept telling me hundreds of times that I was no longer to have this irrational fear of authority. I kept trying to argue with it during that period, and it kept "beating" my resistance down the more I argued. I felt completely helpless physically while I was walking, though I remember experiencing an incredible resistance mentally to whatever was directing me. There was a horrendous pressure all over my body, as though I was encased in this spiritual power, a presence that had as its mission the responsibility to relieve me of this burden, which I had had for over 57 years. I wrestled with this presence until I could no longer resist.

All I know is that after this experience I could not look at the power of others in the same way as I had in the past. My understanding was that I was to tenaciously try to resolve this conflict within my mind, heart and soul. I began to stand up for myself more. I refused to be intimidated, or feel intimidated as I had in the past. I began to self-direct those thoughts toward confident assurance of the ultimate goodwill of others as well as the definitive benevolence of God's institutions of authority on earth. I began to turn it over to Baha'u'llah more often, sincerely telling Him to correct me or send me a lesson that will teach me how to better handle the situation next time.

I was presenting a 10-week program for girls, titled "The Life of the Heroic Girl", for the Rockford Public Library and the YWCA January through March of 2001. One class was particularly difficult for me because I sensed that the library personnel were observing my presentation. Paranoia always set in when I think/imagine that I am being observed. I was concerned that I would be misjudged if I did badly. In retrospect I told myself that may happen! That may not happen! But I told myself that I was doing something that has never been done before and I was allowed to make mistakes. I gave myself authority to make mistakes. I gave myself authority to love that child within that tried so hard to please, with no advocate, no voice, no loving arms to protect her from the intimidation of an unjust authority. Still the paranoia dogged my efforts.

I wrote to my dear friend[24] about my mystical experience. She replied, "I've heard a couple of similar stories along my Baha'i life - I always appreciate hearing of such encounters. I think such

---

[24] Dr. Marilyn Higgins, Personal Correspondence, 2001

stories are truly wonderful. One of my friends had had such encounters that led her to investigate the Faith... and from time to time as she arose to serve the Cause. She talked to Dorothy Baker about it once, and Dorothy Baker said she felt Heaven sometimes brought such experiences to those who might not learn in any other way. She wanted my friend to realize that if she did not continue to have such experiences, it didn't mean heaven had forgotten her, but rather to feel that heaven was confident in her own soul to gain its own strength of discernment through the channels of prayers and the Writings. We should be thankful either way that we receive Guidance. I hope you will collect your mystical experiences and those of others (if possible). I believe they are a subject of interest and do attract people to open themselves to "spiritual susceptibilities". I think that the Baha'i understanding of them is one of the teachings that is unique and attractive in our Faith, as well. We don't deny them, we don't "elevate" them unduly... we accept and process them for what they are worth and for what WE are worth!"

Perhaps this is the first book you have read regarding the Baha'i Faith and the concept of obedience to authority is challenging to you. Are you willing to pick up the challenge and investigate the truth of these claims? Once you begin, you will find yourself on the edge of your seat, drawn further into a deep-seated belief in the power of the Covenant of God to solve mankind's ills.

Chapter Two

Authority of Self Workshop

Empowerment of Women and

Men[25]

South Africa

For Ages Youth through Adult

The Authority of Self Workshop for men and women can be used for many purposes: to assist those who have been rendered powerless by oppression of any form, whether physical abuse, rape, sexual abuse, mental abuse, ethnic or religious intolerance, sexism or racism. Learning and using the concepts in this workshop is as much a part of growing up as learning the three "R's", regardless of oppression.

In addition, it can be used to awaken both men and women to each other's need to develop birth-right power in the context of obedience to a just authority and enable them to walk equally with one another.

---

[25] Please make handouts for #1 through #29 at the end of this workshop from my website above.

Another major purpose is to demonstrate that "Repeated, identical, conscious thoughts (affirmations) physically enlarge the neural circuits in the brain when they are attached to or tagged by positive feelings, which in turn facilitates a change in behavior,"[26] ultimately helping one overcome feelings of despair and anxiety. These repeated, identical, conscious thoughts will be even more powerful if they are preceded by acknowledgments from a mentor who reflects the worth of the oppressed individual.

Authority of Self: A beginning

In preparation for writing my book *Assisting the Traumatized Soul,* I did research through women's literature for several years. The phrase "authority of self" kept popping up. I wondered "What does that mean? Why do the authors not define it?" I did a computer search of Journals and Dissertations at a local University library in the '90's and the phrase was non-existent. Continued research turned up nothing. Finally, I looked up in my thesaurus every word that referred to power that I could find, from energy, faculty, tools, gems, capability, gifts, virtue, power, and such. I found hundreds of references to human birth-right powers in the Revelation of

---

[26] Hal Williamson and Sharon Eakes, "Liberating Greatness: The Whole Brain Guide to An Extraordinary Life", copyright 2006, Word Association Publishers, Pennsylvania, p. 197.

Bahá'u'lláh and defined "authority of self" as a combination of these powers working together, augmenting one another, controlled by each of us in our own lives. I can say with certainty that these powers can be found in other sacred texts and traditions, from Hinduism, Buddhism, Judaism, and Christianity to Islam and the Bahá'í Faith.

I define "Authority of Self" as: the freedom and ability to use birth-right mental powers to make rational and moral choices, self-regulation of the emotions; and the right or permission to act independently with the understanding that one has personal limitations."[27]

Mankind is in need of new powers and virtues, new moralities, new capacities in the day in which we live. They are fully within our grasp, such as the power of speech; the power of choice; the power of discernment; the power of identity; the power of wisdom; the power of intuition; the power of reflection, discovery, and understanding; the power of will, memory, imagination, and freedom to investigate truth; the power of response, anticipation, attention, and receptivity; and the power of reasoning and deduction, induction, acknowledgement, reciprocity and accountability. I have defined each of these powers psychologically and theologically.

---

[27] Phyllis Peterson, "Assisting the Traumatized Soul," copyright 1999, Bahá'í Publishing Trust, Wilmette

Many psychologists and counselors adopt this particular model: Thought generates feeling, which generates behavior or action. This model helps us understand why we do the things we do; explained this way, we can see that it also coincides with the definition of authority of self. Our thoughts about the events of our lives, how others treat us, our losses and our gains, create both positive and negative emotions. But negative emotions can disempower our ability to reason clearly because they affect us biologically.

Oppression also disempowers us. Our oppressor may not allow us to have free speech or freedom of choice. How do we restore balance even when we are being oppressed or simply when things are not going the way we wish they would?

In a talk titled "Obedience to a Higher Being", Ian Semple described the relationship of this to "authority of self" and proposed five simple steps.

1. The first is to accept personal responsibility and accept myself as the ultimate decision maker in my life. (Do all my choices, actions, and responsibility for them come back to me?).

    Every human being has individual endowment, power, and responsibility. Therefore, each person must depend upon their own reason, discernment, and judgment for making decisions and investigating truth.

2. The second step is to recognize personal fallibility (Am I capable of making mistakes because I am not all-knowing and all-wise? Can I admit to myself that my authority is merely a "mortal authority?");

It is wise and mature to confess our helplessness in the face of a Higher Authority in this regard and it marks the culmination of our development.

3. The third step is to recognize a source of authority outside myself, a source of a higher truth (Like a Supreme Being, who is All-Knowing, All-Wise);

Pride and a feeling of superiority can keep us from searching for a higher Authority like Buddha, Allah, God, Krishna, or a Supreme Being who will help us walk a straighter path.

4. The fourth is to understand the requirements of a Just authority that I recognize.

Do we just reap the benefit of the promises of a Just authority or are there expectations/requirements/responsibilities for us to meet and carry out?

5. And the fifth step is the exercise of judgment in carrying out these requirements.

The fact that I am a reasoning human being means that I must judge for myself and carry out these requirements to the best of my ability, which will increase my vision. Then I will be enabled to use "authority of self", my powers, with wisdom and discernment.

A New Definition of Power

Humankind has not always been allowed to use all of its powers, especially women, black men, and Latinos, because power in a male-dominated paradigm, as well as a racist paradigm, has always been used and defined as force. But in the 21st Century, we have a new definition of power. An author by the name of N. Josefowitz defines power as "effectiveness: the ability or capacity to act or perform effectively. This broader concept of power includes the capacity and the ability or competence to get things done by either influencing others or having access to resources. It also includes the idea of granting more autonomy to those with less power.

Power Used as Force

Everyone knows what power used as "force" looks like. We witness it in a world at war today and our history books are littered with the brutality of force.

We also see it in the dangers our children and youth face, early pregnancy, sexual slavery, forced to live on the streets, homeless and motherless, and we see it in the battering of women forced to endure sex and rape with the consequences of HIV/AIDS and ostracism. We also see it in the funerals of HIV/AIDS infected black and white youth and adults world-wide, who could have, but were too stigmatized to ask for help or ARV medication (Anti-Retro Viral medication). Even more disconcerting, we also see power used as force in many kinds of coercive child-rearing techniques: corporal punishment, shaming, blaming. We see it in the economic sphere – people underpaid for their work and forced to acquiesce to lousy work-conditions out of fear of losing even that job and while CEOs live like Caesars. "Education" (schooling) that invests more in testing – threat of bad grades, threat of failure – than in nurturing minds. We see it in law – threat of jail, especially of those who cannot afford impressive legal defense.

Just Authority

Bahá'u'lláh once said, "What mankind needs in this day is obedience unto them that are in authority, and a faithful adherence to the cord of wisdom. The instruments which are essential to the immediate protection, the security and assurance of the human race have been entrusted to the hands, and lie in the grasp, of the governors of human society."[28]

Here is a brief definition of a **just** authority: A rational, nurturing, and just authority treats all as equal with a right to dignity even though others may not have the same power, intellectual capacity, and experience or material status. A just authority, based upon submission to the Creator of us all, helps those under its care discover who they are through steadfast love, tolerance, and non-controlling encouragement. It is the responsibility of **Just** authority to encourage and teach ways of blending individual perspectives because we cannot live without cooperation and reciprocity.

Shared Multiple Perspectives in Community or in a Family:

Living in community requires the yielding of the individual perspective to truth and oneness. "The verbal expression of two or more perspectives requires loving consultation, which includes reconciling the principles of mercy and justice, of freedom and submission, of the sanctity of the right of the individual and of self-surrender, of vigilance, discretion and prudence on the one hand, and fellowship, candour and courage on the other."[29] Then all of us who have been oppressed or who

---

[28] Baha'u'llah, Gleanings from the Writings of Baha'u'llah, Baha'i Publishing Trust, © 1976, p. 206
[29] Shoghi Effendi, Baha'i Administration, p. 7

have oppressed others must then proceed with the utmost devotion, courtesy, dignity, care, and moderation to express our views.

The concept of valid multiple perspectives is foreign to some, because they lived in a family in which there was only one-way communication from higher-to-lower ranked family members. And the belief that a spark of truth could emerge from shared multiple perspectives is even more foreign. The truth that emerges becomes apparent only to the extent that we can link it to the principle of oneness. The important thing is that we share our perspective in two-or- more-way consultation, showing respect for others' viewpoints, trusting that they will show respect for ours.

It's important to remember that self-esteem is not dependent upon instinctively knowing truth without consultation, but on the yielding up of arbitrary perspectives or a treasured opinion that is blocking the truth. We need to know that some will challenge our viewpoint. We don't have to defend it. Some may applaud our viewpoint. That is not a sign that it is a truth for all. And some will be completely indifferent to all perspectives shared. Often, the one person among us who is shaking in his or her shoes in fear of revealing their thoughts may lead us to the spark of truth and oneness or unity we are seeking.

Question: Who is the Authority in your life? How do you discipline yourself?

Our "Authority of Self" regarding morality, for example, can be influenced by media, celebrities, conformity to friends or cultural traditions, pursuit of money, control by boyfriend or girlfriend, or deferring to parental traditions. Questions we can ask ourselves or those who have been disempowered are:

1. How has the influence of the media affected your moral choices as a teenager/adult?
2. How have your personal choices reflected obedience or non-obedience to the commandments of a Higher Power, the police, or your government?
3. Are you your own authority? Or do you give over (abdicate) your authority to your boyfriend, girlfriend, a drug dealer, conform to celebrity standards, or outdated standards and cultural beliefs that are harmful, afraid to stand on your own?
4. Does your spouse/partner participate in multiple sexual partners increasing the possibility of you developing HIV/AIDS or another STD (Sexually Transmitted Disease)?
5. Do you vent a lot because you don't know how to get your powers back or don't believe you have permission to use authority of self? How do you vent and what solutions are there that you see?

6. What is the heart of your personal story? Talk from your own experience and feelings. "I experienced this … " or "I felt this … ", rather than, "They did this. They did that."
7. What have been your experiences with inequality in your family and the culture in which you live?

There are many ways to empower women and men. I have chosen to dismantle a series of negative messages and awaken men and women to affirmations that confront this covert insidious, destructive language that causes despair, anxiety, helplessness, hopelessness and unnecessary rebellion. Instead, I have imbued the following positive messages and higher-thinking affirmations with the powers of "Authority of Self," using the "thought-feeling-action model to rise above the negativity.

Identifying the Negative Messages and Oppressive Language:

Don't be smart or intelligent! Don't ask questions! Don't be close! Don't be weak! Don't be strong! Don't need! Don't be a child! Don't learn and grow! Don't lead! Don't be happy! Don't see from your perspective! Don't be important! Don't be afraid! Don't change! Don't laugh! Don't be different! Don't set boundaries! Don't be aware! Don't be sane! Don't trust! Don't be you! Don't try! Don't talk or express yourself! Don't know yourself! Don't be! Don't take care of yourself! Don't be greedy! Don't make choices! Don't disobey or challenge authority!

This language is in direct opposition to encouraging us to use our birth-right powers: the power of speech, the power of choice, the power of discernment, the power of identity, the power of wisdom, the power of intuition, the power of reflection, discovery, and understanding—also, the power of will, memory, and to search for truth, the power of response, anticipation, attention, and receptivity, the power of accountability, and the power of reasoning, deduction, and to recognize a Higher, Superior Being.

Sometimes the language that imprisons our powers is directed as, "You are lazy! You are stupid! You're crazy! You're BAD! You made me hit you! You are worthless! You're retarded! You whore! You're never going to amount to anything!" No matter how the language is framed, the fundamental relationship is that of disempowerment of the individual's authority of self and destruction of identity. These are "labels" that we internalize; and we believe them to be true. But if we have someone, a friend, parent, therapist, or support group, *that reflects and acknowledges* our good qualities (which should have been done while we were children, by adults) instead of giving us a negative label, we begin to believe in ourselves. Our true identity becomes strongly resistant to external criticism, or a victim to pathological self-criticism. Further, we begin to know how to "affirm" our good qualities which the following exercises will illustrate.[30]

Feelings:
Feelings are very important to this exercise because if we have been disempowered, our feelings are going to be negative. This can result in depression and/or a loss of a feeling of nobility. Our thoughts are going to be negative, too, and they, together, will negate our ability to change our behavior. There is much research that has been done on how to change how our brain thinks. *In Liberating Greatness: The Whole Brain Guide to An Extraordinary Life*, authors Hal Williamson and Sharon Eakes say that an "affirmation when tagged/combined with positive emotions create strong, new neural circuits" in the brain. "These new circuits have the capacity to alter old, unwanted behaviors in favor of new, desired behaviors"[31] because they lift us up out of the despair, paving the way for new thoughts which enhance our esteem and nobility.

Right now, think of the happiest moment you've ever experienced in your life! It may be a moment when you have achieved or accomplished a goal, the birth of a baby, the feeling you had when you learned to drive and became more independent;

---

[30] Dr. David Burns, "Feeling Good: 10 Cognitive Distortions that can cause depression.
[31] Hal Williamson and Sharon Eakes, *Liberating Greatness*, copyright 2006, Word Association Publishers, Pennsylvania, p. 197

when someone saw the real you and accepted you. At any rate, it is an "I can do it!" moment that brought you great joy! Bring up the memory of it, then bring up the "Feeling" you had. What Mr. Williamson suggests is that you take that special, positive feeling and tag, connect, mark, or attach it to your new affirmation. This will create the strong neural circuits that will help you alter your old, unwanted behaviors and emotions. Whatever challenge you are experiencing needs to be tagged emotionally with that joyous feeling, instead of the feelings of disempowerment that weigh you down. When the negative thoughts repeatedly come up, as they always have, use the following affirmations and tag them with the invincible feeling of joy! Doing it repeatedly will actually change your brain, given time! Repeat the affirmation "identically" three times, or craft your own affirmation, but remember to tag it with a positive emotion while you do so!

There are actually "twin concepts" to adopt to win the battle: Tag the affirmation with the positive emotion; and "detach" your mind and heart from the negative emotion. Becoming detached actually opens you up to a myriad of positive and wonderful emotions.

Go through this list of 29 negative messages and positive affirmations as a group, selecting 5 or 6 that apply to your situation, depending on the size of the group. Divide into groups of two. Because each of us is dependent upon a caregiver for the development of our identity, partner #1 will look directly into your eyes with compassion and gentleness, reflecting and acknowledging your identity in a positive way. Partner #2 will say the affirmation three times and each time consciously try to increase his or her feelings of joy and faith:

Discuss the times you have listened to the negative messages automatically, without being aware of the accompanying feelings and without challenging the messages by tagging the affirmation with a positive feeling. Think of the affirmation as a celebration of "higher thinking." Know that even if you have no resources or if violence surrounds you, emotionally tagging your positive/past experience with its remembered feeling of joy, will help you to become detached, and able to use your power of reasoning.

The reason for having you partner with a "Mentor" who acknowledges you is because they are the advocate you should have had as a child who was to be there to reflect your wholesomeness and assist you to develop your true identity. Babies look with longing at their mother's face and are dependent on those peaceful moments of reflection. If you did not get that, it doesn't mean that this process is gone forever. You can grasp for it today with trust, with acknowledgement confirming your affirmation.

The following acknowledgements and affirmations grant you your birthright powers of

Authority of Self. Repeat each acknowledgement and affirmation three times:

1. Don't be smart or intelligent! You're stupid!

Q. What feelings and thoughts about yourself would prevent you from revealing that you are smart or intelligent?

Partner #1: (Look directly and with compassion into your partner's eyes for one minute before you speak): "I acknowledge that you are an intelligent person. You don't have to pretend to be stupid with men, women, or authority. I encourage you to develop the power of independent investigation of truth today. You can discover a new reality with your power of reasoning, and feel joy while you do so!"

Partner #2: (Look directly and with acceptance and trust into your partner's eyes for one minute before you speak): "I challenge the belief that I have to pretend to be stupid with men, women, or authority. Today I will look for ways to reveal instead of conceal my intelligence. I will develop the power of independent investigation of truth. I will discover a new reality with my power of reasoning by bringing my inner thoughts into public view. I will speak my truth without fear. I celebrate my visible intelligence. I tag this affirmation, these new thoughts, with a feeling of joy that comes from a memory of a prior accomplishment! And I repeat this affirmation word for word, knowing it will lead to a change in my behavior!" (Feel the joy you remember and then say the affirmation three times with that feeling of joy glued into every word!)

2. Don't ask questions!
Q. What feelings would prevent you from asking questions?
Partner #1: (Look directly and with compassion into your partner's eyes for one minute before you speak): "I feel sad that you have been prevented from asking questions in the past, but I encourage you to seek out people who are 'safe' and ask them questions. Ask them how they overcame their fear. I acknowledge that asking questions is a birthright power that can lead you to equality with others as well as learning truth. Asking questions is a ladder to knowledge. I believe that you can do it with safe people without fear of violence."

Partner #2: (Look directly and with acceptance and trust into your partner's eyes for one minute before you speak): "I challenge my belief that I will experience violence if I ask questions. Asking questions now becomes my basis for searching for reality or truth. Consciously developing the power of independent investigation of truth means I don't have to blindly obey authority or follow tradition and culture exclusively. I celebrate my birthright power to question. I attach a feeling of courage and curiosity to this affirmation; and I do it repeatedly!!" (Repeat this affirmation two more times.)

3. Don't be close!

Q. What feelings do you have when someone tries to get close to you?

Partner # 1: (Look directly and with compassion into your partner's eyes for one minute before you speak): "I acknowledge that unity, friendship, and relationship are gifts that are given to us regardless of whether our family of origin is troubled; and I believe you are capable of forming close bonds with safe people. I encourage you to call a community member, write a note, and enter into a reciprocal relationship, one in which personal, sexual, emotional, spatial, and energy boundaries will be respected."

Partner #2: (Look directly and with acceptance and trust into your partner's eyes for one minute before you speak): "I challenge the belief that I have to be totally independent or that I am not lovable because I am different than my siblings or my peers. I no longer have to do everything all by myself. I can observe varying degrees of development, perfection, and consciousness and determine who is safe to be close to and who is not. Clarifying the limits of acceptable behavior will allow me to be close to others and experience safety. I tag this affirmation with the feeling of joy that comes from decisiveness because I can tell others what I need and want, offering the same to them. I repeat this affirmation identically, marking it with a feeling of previously remembered joy." (Repeat this affirmation two more times.)

4. Don't be weak/strong! You weakling!

Q. What feelings tell you that you have to be weak or strong?

Partner #1: (Look directly and with compassion into your partner's eyes for one minute before you speak): "I acknowledge that you have been raised to think you have to be weak and dependent in the face of challenges ... or strong at all times. I encourage you to know that all of us have human frailties. This does not mean you are a weakling. Believe that you don't have to play out the roles that have been assigned to you. You don't have to cower in front of anyone ... weak or strong."

Partner #2: (Look directly and with acceptance and trust into your partner's eyes for one minute before you speak.) "I challenge the belief that I should be a superwoman or superman. Today I perceive weakness as vital to understanding my relationship to a Superior Being who is All-Powerful. I no longer have to tough it out and hide all my human frailties. Using the power of will I can let go of the role I have accepted and the mask of strength I wear. I will begin to trust that I will be accepted for who I am in moments of weakness as well as strength. I can allow myself to cry when I feel sad or frustrated, but I promise myself to rejoice after the tears because it will help me detach from the sadness.   I feel successful; and I will no longer allow myself to cower in front of anyone. I emotionally attach a feeling of joy continuously while I repeat this affirmation word for word identically." (Repeat this affirmation two more times.)

5. Don't need! You're so needy, you're

pathetic!

Q. What feelings do you have when you

sense that you have a need?

Partner #1: (Look directly and with compassion into your partner's eyes for one minute before you speak.) "I acknowledge to you that when a person's needs are unmet in childhood, it causes them to postpone indefinitely meeting their own needs as adults. It also causes them to believe they are undeserving. I encourage you to seek to acquire your moderate needs and if the scale tips and you reach out for something extra, I hope that you will not self-punish. Just recognize it as an attempt at 'need-fulfillment' and go on to establish a balance next time."

Partner #2: (Look directly and with acceptance and trust into your partner's eyes for one minute before you speak.) "I challenge my belief that I am undeserving, that I must continually martyr myself, or that I must self-punish when I need something. I will speak my needs and the needs of others. I will use the power of will to overcome the feeling of inertia or apathy that prevents me from acquiring my moderate needs, whether they be material or spiritual, energy, or space, time or emotional. I celebrate the power to ask to have my needs met; and I repeatedly tag this affirmation with the feeling of reassurance and joy, both for myself and others." (Repeat this affirmation two more times.)

6. Don't be a child!

Q. What feelings prevent you from being child-like?

Partner #1: (Look directly and with compassion into your partner's eyes for one minute before you speak.) "I will acknowledge to you that all of us have an inner child that must have expression in play—whether that is through music, dance, art, writing, photography, or anything that helps us get beyond caretaking to celebrating life with joy. I encourage you to capture the creativity that lies within you as a gift that you can give to yourself."

Partner #2: (Look directly and with acceptance and trust into your partner's eyes for one minute before you speak.) "All of us have a child within and so do I. I challenge the belief that I must always work and should never play or be spontaneous. I will advocate for my inner child. I will become more aware of the power of my identity to firmly know who I am, what is important to me and where I fit in this world. I will not settle for the rigid role of caretaker that was assigned to me as a child. I can give care willingly and also take care of myself. I celebrate my ability to satisfy the needs of my inner child and the adult that

I am because I am multi-faceted. I continuously tag this affirmation with the feeling of playfulness and confidence." (Repeat this affirmation two more times.)

7. Don't learn and grow!

Q.   What feelings prevent you from seeking out knowledge?

Partner #1: (Look directly and with compassion into your partner's eyes for one minute before you speak.) "I acknowledge that you are capable of growing and developing the gems of knowledge within you, as well as digging deep into the collective knowledge of humankind. I encourage you to listen to your power of intuition, which is strong in women, and can be developed in men, for it will confirm the pathway you choose to knowledge."

Partner #2: (Look directly and with acceptance and trust into your partner's eyes for one minute before you speak.) "I challenge the belief that I have to fit the mold prescribed for me by authority figures. This week I will turn toward the source of my inner knowledge, my power of intuition. I will educate myself to discover the gems of knowledge within me. Though I have often felt discounted and discouraged, I celebrate new success in my capacity to grasp knowledge, my power to discover something new. I emotionally mark this affirmation with the feeling of inquisitiveness that has guided me and helped confirm my intuition; and I do it repeatedly with a feeling of joy." (Repeat this affirmation two more times.)

8. Don't lead!

Q. What feelings hold you back from showing others how capable you are?
Partner #1: (Look directly and with compassion into your partner's eyes for one minute before you speak.) "I acknowledge that you are fully capable of making decisions, and that you have both leadership capacity and the ability to be an active participant. I encourage you to choose a mentor or to be your own mentor in the process of changing and growing."

Partner #2: (Look directly and with acceptance and trust into your partner's eyes for one minute before you speak.) "I challenge the belief that I have to be less than capable in order to escape the wrath of authority. I challenge the belief that I have to be passive and compliant while other people make decisions. I no longer have to be a follower only. I can take the lead or be an active participant using my power of receptivity and response. I celebrate bold action and with my power of identity, I change and grow. At this point of my development I would not feel shame, but would welcome a mentor who would teach me servant/leadership skills. I emotionally attach a feeling of courage to this affirmation. I repeatedly combine this affirmation with the feeling of courage, joy, and determination." (Repeat this affirmation two more times.)

9. Don't be happy!

Q. What feelings squelch your happiness and spontaneity?

Partner #1: (Look directly and with compassion into your partner's eyes for one minute before you speak.) "I acknowledge that you were created to experience happiness and nobility, and that you can now reach out for it. I encourage you to be spontaneous and to find people you can laugh and play with, for drawing near to others in oneness, reciprocity, and co-operation are some of the reasons you were created."

Partner #2: (Look directly and with acceptance and trust into your partner's eyes for one minute before you speak.) "I challenge my belief that I have to be emotionally sober and duty-bound at all times. I can be spontaneous. I can allow myself to laugh and play instead of rigidly sticking to the list of things I need to complete. I can sing, dance, and listen to music. I can also achieve spiritual happiness by seeking out things that will give my life meaning. I celebrate the ultimate happiness: drawing closer to my Creator. I repeatedly and identically tag this affirmation with the feelings of happiness and spontaneity!"(Repeat this affirmation two more times.)

10. Don't see!

Q. When does the feeling of confusion cloud your perception of the truth?
Partner #1: (Look directly and with compassion into your partner's eyes for one minute before you speak.) "I acknowledge that in the past your family of origin caused confusion as you witnessed such crazy-making behaviors and messages as: 'I love you. / Leave me alone.' I encourage you to find a neutral party to speak your truth to and have it validated so you can stop minimizing the great stress it has and is causing you to feel."

Partner #2: (Look directly and with acceptance and trust into your partner's eyes for one minute before you speak.) "I challenge my belief that the truth is too painful to experience. When things are not going well in my relationships and I experience confusion or crazy-making behavior, I can test out my perceptions with a neutral party. I don't have to minimize the effects of others' treatment of me or rationalize excuses for others' behavior. I celebrate as I perceive the truth and speak the truth. I emotionally attach a feeling of peacefulness and courage to this affirmation every time I want to express the truth of my experience. I also connect a feeling of freedom to this affirmation repeatedly." (Repeat this affirmation two more times.)

11. Don't be important! You are worthless! You'll never amount to anything!

Q.   Where does your feeling of

worthlessness come from?

Partner #1: (Look directly and with compassion into your partner's eyes for one minute before you speak.) "I acknowledge the personal worth, dignity, and nobility that is inherent within you. I admire the peace and unity you bring to your community, for that is what has made you achieve a noble station. I encourage you to remember the confidence and amazement you felt when someone in the past has advocated for you. Know that more advocates and mentors will affirm your value as you journey on."

Partner #2: (Look directly and with acceptance and trust into your partner's eyes for one minute before you speak.) "I challenge my belief and the emotional feeling I have that I am worthless. My value does not come from measurable achievement or having money. It comes from my ability to love, from the justice with which I treat others, from the unity and peace I alone bring to my personal relationships or my community. I celebrate my nobility and dignity whether I do the work of a laborer or preside over a company. In either case, I am merely my Creator's servant. I tag this affirmation with the feeling of relief and confidence that I have experienced when someone advocated for me in the past, and I do it repeatedly!" (Repeat this affirmation two more times.)

12. Don't be afraid! (or) You coward!!

Q. What acts in the past have made you feel brave? What person makes you feel brave?
Partner #1: (Look directly and with compassion into your partner's eyes for one minute before you speak.) "I acknowledge that the fact that you are living is a testimony of your courage and bravery, having gone

through all the trials that you have. I encourage you to celebrate your courage and use it to make healthy changes, even if it means that you have to formulate new friendships. Look forward with joy!"

Partner #2: (Look directly and with acceptance and trust into your partner's eyes for one minute before you speak.) "I challenge the belief that I am a coward. With a healthy fear of a Higher Being, which teaches me to obey JUST institutions of authority, I no longer need fear any one. I celebrate courage. Through the power of faith, I can take risks to make healthy changes in my life. I repeatedly tag this affirmation with the feeling of courage and security with every cell of my body and brain; and I repeat this affirmation identically each time fear comes up." (Repeat this affirmation two more times.)

13. Don't change!

Q. What feelings are so strong that they keep you from expressing your true identity? Who gives you "Change back!!" messages when you have tried to change?

Partner # 1: (Look directly and with compassion into your partner's eyes for one minute before you speak.) "I acknowledge that change is difficult, whether it is in your beliefs, job, relationships, or values. I also acknowledge that others may be uncomfortable when you take a different direction than they do. I encourage you to stay the course and accept their limitations, making choices that are right for you."

Partner #2: (Look directly and with acceptance and trust into your partner's eyes for one minute before you speak.) "I challenge the belief that I have to be passive and compliant while others make healthy changes in their value systems, beliefs, jobs, and relationships. If others are uncomfortable with the changes I make, I can still bring my true identity into focus and wait for them to adjust to the change. If they cannot make the adjustment, I can accept their limitations while staying on my course of growth. I celebrate my right to choose and have a self-determined life while observing the Covenant of God, which sets spiritual, physical, and moral limits for me. I visualize not only new growth, but connect the virtues of Faith and Patience to it repeatedly as I say this affirmation word for word." (Repeat this affirmation two more times.)

14. Don't laugh!

Q. Are you afraid to have such positive emotions as hope, faith, and love? Are you afraid to laugh, or that people will laugh at you?

Partner # 1: (Look directly and with compassion into your partner's eyes for one minute before you speak.) "I acknowledge for you that laughter is a very healthy action and response to the contrasts of life and our own foibles. It is cruelty when it is used to ridicule others. I encourage you to celebrate happy occasions and the full range of your positive emotions such as faith, hope, and love."

Partner #2: (Look directly and with acceptance and trust into your partner's eyes for one minute before you speak.) "I challenge my belief that people laugh only to ridicule my body, my thoughts, or my speech. I now celebrate the joy that laughter can bring to happy occasions. I also celebrate the full range of my positive emotions such as hope, faith, love, determination, purpose, festivity, and a strong will to live. Tears also become an important release of frustration and anger and become a signal to me that I may need to address a need or confront a wrong-doer. Emotionally I return to that moment in time when I did have hope and I connect that hope to this affirmation so that I will experience a full range of positive emotions." (Repeat this affirmation two more times.)

15. Don't be different!

Q. Guilt is a powerful emotion. Does it stop you from trying new things, or taking a new approach to life as you appear to be different from friends and relatives?

Partner #1: (Look directly and with compassion into your partner's eyes for one minute before you speak.) "I acknowledge your individuality in developing your gifts, your thoughts, and your character. I encourage you to try new things and to try a new approach to life, free of guilt, because we all live by grace and mercy as we develop our virtues of trustworthiness, forgiveness, love, and compassion."

Partner #2: (Look directly and with acceptance and trust into your partner's eyes for one minute before you speak.) "I now challenge the belief that I have to be the same as everyone around me. If my thoughts, character, and the way that I dress set me apart from others, I can celebrate my individuality as I add variety to my relationships and environment. I will no longer allow my differentness to be swallowed up by convention and tradition or guilt that others try to heap upon me. Some things will always remain the same, such as the fact that rights always come with responsibilities; but I will conquer my guilt with the feeling of

Freedom with which I mark this affirmation repeatedly and intentionally." (Repeat this affirmation two more times.)

16. Don't set boundaries!

Q. Your internal alarm is a combination of negative feelings that cause confusion and can immobilize you. Have you recognized it in the past? What is it like for you?

Partner #1: (Look directly and with compassion into your partner's eyes for one minute before you speak.) "I acknowledge that many people are either depressed because of violations of their boundaries, or they isolate themselves, further increasing their depression, and feel angry because others treat them as an object. I encourage you to take control of issues regarding your sexuality, energy, money, time, and emotions so that you and others can glimpse the real you."

Partner #2: (Look directly and with acceptance and trust into your partner's eyes for one minute before you speak.) "I challenge my belief that it is too risky to set boundaries with others. I am not the property of others or an object to be used as others please. I celebrate my freedom from boundary enmeshment (violation). I celebrate my internal alarm that tells me something is wrong and needs to be set right before my relationship proceeds. I now take control of and practice vigilance for the boundaries that govern my thinking, spirituality, emotions, will, perceptions, sexuality, money, time, space, energy, body, and belongings. With the virtue of vigilance, I tag this affirmation and set boundaries with others repeatedly until they begin to know who I am—my reality. The end result of this is that my identity will become clear to me." (Repeat this affirmation two more times.)

17. Don't be aware!

Q. **Some people minimize their emotional pain, saying, "Oh, it's not that bad." Or they rationalize the behavior of others by saying "Oh, he was drunk, otherwise he wouldn't have done that." Give examples from your own life.**

Partner #1: (Look directly and with compassion into your partner's eyes for one minute before you speak.) "I acknowledge that minimizing your emotional pain and rationalizing the behaviors of others is a way of denying your awareness of boundary violations. I encourage you to stay in the present, rather than go into a trance, in order to grow into greater emotional and mental health."

Partner # 2: (Look directly and with acceptance and trust into your partner's eyes for one minute before you speak.) "I challenge my belief that it is too painful to be confronted with reality and truth. I allow myself to become conscious of the defense mechanisms that prevent me from being fully aware of my denial, the times I minimize my emotional pain and rationalize the behaviors of others; I take responsibility for my dissociation (going into a trance) and its consequences. I celebrate my growing awareness that protects me because it keeps me in the present, where I can choose relationships that are healthy instead of harmful. I repeatedly connect the feeling of gratitude to this affirmation and repeatedly affirm my consciousness, knowing it will lead to new behaviors." (Repeat this affirmation two more times.)

18. Don't be sane!

Q. Do people in your life allow you to have access to the truth of your history? Explain further.

Partner #1: (Look directly and with compassion into your partner's eyes for one minute before you speak.) "I acknowledge that unhealthy family dynamics may have prevented your having access to the truth of your history. I encourage you to step outside the limiting roles that have been forced upon you and communicate your truth and past with courage."

Partner #2: (Look directly and with acceptance and trust into your partner's eyes for one minute before you speak.) "I challenge the belief that I have to seek the safety of a fantasy world and live in denial. I celebrate the independent investigation of truth which will rid me of that which is false—the roles I have been forced to play, the perceptions that were discounted by others, the thwarting (blocking) of my attempts to communicate my intelligence through speech or feelings. I also celebrate having access to the truth of my history, for that is the root of my sanity, even though it may be painful, yet I have determined to not live in the past. I mark this affirmation repeatedly with the feeling of determination, combining intuition and truth to live my life fearlessly in the present to change the future." (Repeat this affirmation two more times.)

19. Don't trust!

Q. Do you trust your perceptions, feelings, and thoughts regarding who is trustworthy? What has happened in the past

when you have or have not trusted? What did it feel like?

Partner #1: (Look directly and with compassion into your partner's eyes for one minute before you speak.) "I acknowledge that you have the right to exercise all of the component powers of 'authority of self', so that others do not control you. I encourage you to trust your perceptions, feelings, and thoughts regarding who is trustworthy and who is not."

Partner #2: (Look directly and with acceptance and trust into your partner's eyes for one minute before you speak.) "I challenge my belief that I have to control everyone and everything in my life. I celebrate the component powers of 'authority of self', within the guidelines of Justice. This makes it possible for me to trust and give up my need to control others and always be defending myself. I now trust my power of perception, feelings, and thoughts that help me come to a conclusion about who is trustworthy and who is not to be trusted. I am no longer open to boundary enmeshment or violation. I repeatedly connect this affirmation with the feeling of trust and joy, combined with caution, knowing that all three are virtues meant to protect me." (Repeat this affirmation two more times.)

19. Don't be you!

Q. Everyone has multiple roles to play in life. Do you have a role that is too rigid, in which others control you? How does it make you feel?

Partner #1: (Look directly and with compassion into your partner's eyes for one minute before you speak.) "I acknowledge that your identity is a very precious thing and that it is continually evolving as you learn from the collective knowledge of humankind and sacred texts. I encourage you to expand your noble identity beyond the rigid roles that you accepted before you had enough life experience to realize that they were unhealthy."

Partner #2: (Look directly and with acceptance and trust into your partner's eyes for one minute before you speak.) "I challenge my belief that I have to play a role or have permission to be the person I really am. I no longer allow myself to be affected when others ridicule, discount, ignore, manipulate, or try to control who I am. I celebrate my inmost true self, which is a trust from my Creator, and which was created in His image as noble and full of beauty. I follow my true purpose, now, and that is to develop virtues, and know the sacred aspects of life. I repeatedly connect the feelings of boldness and spontaneity, which I remember from my past, to this affirmation, no longer dependent and powerless." (Repeat this affirmation two more times.)

21. Don't try!

Q. Do you feel like giving up when you don't have cooperation and reciprocity coming from others? What could you do instead?

Partner #1: (Look directly and with compassion into your partner' eyes for one minute before you speak.) "I acknowledge that in spite of (or because of) your family history, you inherited the Herculean task of not only trying to rise above your trauma, but also trying to please those who were never satisfied, were uncooperative, and would not reciprocate. I encourage you to seek out friends who will be cooperative and extend reciprocity to you. Be assured that they are out there!"

Partner #2: (Look directly and with acceptance and trust into your partner's eyes for one minute before you speak.) "I challenge my belief that life is too hard to keep trying. I challenge my feeling that I'll never be able to please anyone no matter what I do. I rekindle my desire for cooperation and reciprocity. With my power of faith I begin anew to make efforts toward my goals whether they relate to my work or my personal life. I now celebrate my power of speech, my power of will, and my desire to rise above the trauma in my life. I repeatedly attach the feeling of success and joy to this affirmation because I know I am cooperative and that I reciprocate at appropriate times." (Repeat this affirmation two more times.)

22. Don't talk!

Q. Have you ever had your feelings and thoughts reflected by others? What did it feel like?

Partner #1: (Look directly and with compassion into your partner's eyes for one minute before you speak.) "I acknowledge that you may never have had someone to share your feelings and thoughts with in open, direct, and honest consultation. But try to remember at least one person who has advocated for you. I encourage you to imagine that he or she is here before you while you release your feelings and thoughts, no longer silent.

Partner #2: (Look directly and with acceptance and trust into your partner's eyes for one minute before you speak.) "I challenge my belief that I must remain silent, refrain from expressing my thoughts and opinions or refrain from confronting others with my power of speech. I challenge my belief that open, direct, honest discussion or consultation is too risky. I no longer fear the threat of violence if I should talk. I can ask to have my feelings and thoughts reflected by others who are safe. I can ask for validation. I can offer my viewpoint and show respect for others' views without discounting my own views. I celebrate release from oppressive force that kept me silent all these years. I repeatedly mark this affirmation with the feeling of freedom to speak that I remember from my past. If I never had that feeling of freedom, then I choose the feeling of gratitude and happiness for that one person I remember who advocated for me and my voice, utilizing that as a key freedom." (Repeat this affirmation two more times.)

23. Don't know yourself.

Q. Do you feel like you are the only one in the world who makes mistakes and therefore, you shame, blame, crucify, and guilt yourself every day? Explain.

Partner #1:   Look directly and with compassion into your partner's eyes for one minute before you speak.) "I acknowledge that there is no one person on earth who is perfect and has never made a mistake. Self-criticism is the hardest of habits to break, and compassion for others comes easily. I encourage you to now extend compassion to yourself instead of shaming, blaming, and crucifying yourself every day."

Partner #2: (Look directly and with acceptance and trust into your partner's eyes for one minute before you speak.) "I challenge my belief that I cannot put aside the roles that have been assigned to me and discover my true identity. I challenge my belief that my world will fall apart and others will be uncomfortable if I seek to know my inmost true self through the awkward process of elimination that a teenager goes through as part of her or his development. I release myself from shaming, blaming, and guilt when I make mistakes. But I turn toward the Sacred Texts of my Creator for guidance and using 'authority of self', take responsibility for the consequences of all my choices. I celebrate the unveiling of the ever-evolving self that I am beginning to know. I repeatedly attach the feeling of compassion for myself that I have experienced in the past, and gratitude of knowing that others, too, have had compassion for me when I have made mistakes." (Repeat this affirmation two more times.)

24. Don't be!

Q. Nobility is not only a virtue ... it's a feeling as well. What kinds of behavior help you feel noble?

Partner #1: (Look directly and with compassion into your partner's eyes for one minute before you speak.) "I acknowledge that you have been created noble and encourage you to seek out that which will lead you to self-worth and nobility. This will be found in the purposeful things that you do and the service you render to your Creator and to humankind. Purposeful service to others helps expand our noble birthright, enabling us to feel our dignity."

Partner #2: (Look directly and with acceptance and trust into your partner's eyes for one minute before you speak.) "I challenge my belief that I am not enough as a child, a woman, a man, a friend, a spouse, or an employee. I reclaim my identity as a child of my Creator. I no longer have to continually do something spectacular to be accepted. Yet I can seek to know that which leads me to self-worth and nobility, or that which leads me to shame. I celebrate the fact that a Supreme Being created my soul with His light within, and I claim nobility as my birthright. I recreate that feeling of nobility in my heart that I felt when I gave of myself to the Cause of Justice and the Greater Good; and I attach that feeling repeatedly to this affirmation." (Repeat this affirmation two more times.)

25. Don't think!

Q. Does problem-solving by yourself make you feel like you are going in circles? That's called being locked into your own perspective. Who could you trust in asking for feedback or to validate your powers?

Partner #1: (Look directly and with compassion into your partner's eyes for one minute before you speak.) "I acknowledge that it can seem difficult to find someone you could trust for feedback on problems, validation of your powers, or simply to vent emotions that distract you from discovering your own perspective I encourage you to communicate your thoughts and feelings confidently with a safe person who encourages you to problem-solve."

Partner #2: (Look directly and with acceptance and trust into your partner's eyes for one minute before you speak.) "I challenge my belief that it is threatening to think. I no longer have to drift into a fantasy world when things go wrong. I can stay in the here and now to problem-solve, to ask questions, to communicate my feelings, thoughts, history, and hopes, to ask for feedback, validation, and guidance. I celebrate my powers of reasoning and understanding, for they are spiritual gifts from my Creator. I repeatedly connect the feeling of confidence to this affirmation, knowing that a mentor, if asked, would help me problem-solve by pointing out to me my unique powers, thus empowering me." (Repeat this affirmation two more times.)

26. Don't like yourself!

Q. Do you have an internalized voice that says, "You are bad?" Whenever you hear a "YOU" message like that, know that it was imposed originally by an external source. Who gave you messages like that when you were a child?

Partner #1: (Look directly and with compassion into your partner's eyes for one minute before you speak.) "I acknowledge that 'YOU' messages are not part of your permanent identity. They came from an external source—and you were too young to deflect them. Long after that external source was gone, you adopted these messages as your own. I encourage you to free yourself from them and from the self-criticism that results from them."

Partner #2: (Look directly and with acceptance and trust into your partner's eyes for one minute before you speak.) "I challenge myself that I have to abuse myself every time I make a mistake. I challenge the belief that I have to listen to an internalized, abusive voice that has haunted me from childhood. It tells me I am bad, but I don't have to own its judgment of me. I no longer have to compare myself to others, but justly seek to do my best whatever my goal. I celebrate my freedom from constant criticism and punishment, whether by self or others. I repeatedly connect the feeling of excellence in a job well done, creating pride and joy that I remember from my past; because nobility is the way I was created. I detach myself from 'you' messages such as. 'You are stupid', which I have learned from an external source." (Repeat this affirmation two more times.)

27. Don't be greedy! You are so selfish!

Q. We need material as well as spiritual bounties. What needs are you thirsting for, and what feelings do you have when you try to fulfill those needs?
Partner # 1: (Look directly and with compassion into your partner's eyes for one minute before you speak.) "I acknowledge

that the true bounties are 'spiritual' and are meant to support our material needs. I encourage you to celebrate the material as well as the spiritual wealth that a loving, merciful, bountiful Creator has in store for you."

Partner #2: (Look directly and with acceptance and trust into your partner's eyes for one minute before you speak.) "I challenge my belief that to 'need' is to be greedy or selfish. I can fulfill my need for food, clothing, love, and attention without labeling myself as a greedy person. I allow bounties of my Creator to build trust and pride and hope within my heart and mind. I allow my needs to become conscious. I celebrate the material as well as the spiritual wealth that a loving, merciful, bountiful Creator bestows upon me. I repeatedly connect the feeling of contentment and joy with the will of a Supreme Being with this affirmation, knowing that He provides me with both material and spiritual bounties." (Repeat this affirmation two more times.)

28. Don't make choices!

Q. What has happened to you in the past when you tried to assert your power of choice? What feelings do you have when you come to the point of making a choice?

Partner # 1: (Look directly and with compassion into your partner's eyes for one minute before you speak.) "Did you know that babies are not passive and compliant? Did you know that there was a time that you explored your small world, making choice after choice, until you were overly criticized and lost the ability to assert yourself? I encourage you to celebrate freedom from oppression, knowing that freedom does come with responsibilities and consequences for your choices."

Partner #2: (Look directly and with acceptance and trust into your
partner's eyes for one minute before you speak.) "I challenge my belief that I must be passive and compliant instead of a choice-maker. I challenge my belief that I must conform to escape the criticism of others or my own self-punishment. I now choose to assert myself and my identity. I now choose to be different, to have higher thoughts, to develop virtues that set me aside for my true purpose. I can say 'This is who I am!' and respect the differences of others. I am no longer afraid of my power of choice or volition. I celebrate it as freedom from oppression. I now celebrate taking responsibility for the consequences of my choices, knowing that ultimately I am

responsible to my Creator for the choices that I make. I repeatedly tag this affirmation with the feeling of enthusiasm and joy because it uplifts my soul as I make hopeful and moral choices." (Repeat this affirmation two more times.)

29. Don't disobey or challenge "authority!"

Q. What has happened to you emotionally when you have blindly obeyed authority in the past? How can you break free of this injustice and use "Authority of Self" to regulate your emotions, and act with the power of discernment?

Partner #1: (Look directly and with compassion into your partner's eyes for one minute before you speak.) "I acknowledge that you have been encouraged to blindly obey authority, and that has resulted in emotional and mental oppression. But you cannot find safety in blind obedience or by abdicating your powers. I encourage you to utilize 'Authority of Self' as you search to recognize those truths that are universal and that lead us to service for the Greater Good."

Partner #2: (Look directly and with acceptance and trust into your partner's eyes for one minute before you speak.) "I challenge the belief that blindly following authority is the safest way to live my life. I challenge the belief that I must blindly obey regardless of the content or context of the issue. I refuse to discount my own search for truth, my own inner vision, or invalidate my ability to recognize the truth I discover. I now celebrate 'Authority of Self' bestowed upon me by a loving, just, and merciful Creator, to be used for the Greater Good. And I celebrate my spiritual power of perception that assists me in recognizing truth. I repeatedly mark this affirmation with the feeling of gratitude and joy I have felt in the past, grateful that I know right from wrong, good from bad, and that I have the Sacred Texts to guide me." (Repeat this affirmation two more times.)

Create your own Affirmations with the powers that make up the Authority of Self. Make it <u>a time-limited action statement.</u>

"I challenge my belief that I must remain silent in the face of the unjust anger or criticism of others. This week I will use the power of <u>   speech   </u> to speak up for myself when someone criticizes me. Though I may normally be silent, this time I will defend myself, but I will speak kindly. I also know that I do not have to speak kindly to a tyrant or an oppressor. I may feel like withdrawing, hiding, or running away because I am afraid, but I will stand my ground and speak my truth. I repeatedly connect the feeling of safety and joy with this affirmation."

"I challenge my belief that I cannot tell people who I am and what I need, distinguishing myself from them. This week I will recognize my power of _____identity_____ and express my opinions, what I want, and what I need with freedom. I will tell at least two people what I need; and I will share my opinions with two people. I may feel timid because I'm not used to telling people what I want and need. I may have to reinforce my statements 3 to 5 times again and again; but I will stand firm. I repeatedly tag this affirmation with the feeling of courage that I have experienced even at one moment in time."

"I challenge my belief that I have to numb my feelings. This week I will use my power ____of speech____ to speak my **feelings** of anger, resentment, and outrage when someone discounts my feelings or memories of the past, or when they do not treat me as if I am equal to them. I also know that 'venting' these emotions is not problem-solving. I can prepare myself for this in the privacy of my home and make angry faces in the mirror, growling noises in my throat as I express my feelings, and yet regulate my feelings so that when I confront the person who is treating me as 'less-than', I will still retain my dignity. I repeatedly attach the feeling of justice to this affirmation; and if I have never experienced justice in my history, I will choose serenity as I act with nobility."

(Examples of feelings: Anger, resentment, perturbed, unhappy, joyful, glad, sad, disappointed, ticked off, excited, glum, hopeful, disillusioned, patient, mixed-up, conflicted, and others.)

Questions and Answers: 10 to 15 minutes

Authority of Self:
Here is the definition of authority of self again: "Authority of Self" is the freedom and ability to use God-given mental powers to make rational and moral choices, self-regulation of the emotions; and the right or permission to act independently with the understanding that one has personal limitations. Remember, the model is: "I think! I feel! I investigate truth and reality. (I then regulate my emotions.) I act!"

There are a total of 29 negative messages that are combined with positive affirmations to lift one up and demonstrate how to use the powers of authority of self to achieve balance, well-being, and greatness.

The next chapter, Chapter Three, represents a "coming of age ceremony," a rite of passage for a girl who has reached the age of maturity, 15 years old. Her parents want her to recognize the fact that she has human rights and birthright powers that must be developed in obedience to the Covenant of God. They have bestowed these powers upon her from childhood to maturity, incrementally as she has shown responsibility and cooperation. And with this rite of passage, they grant her full autonomy.

Chapter Three

The Chalice of Power, (Emily's Coming of Age Ceremony)

A Story for Youth

that serves as a beautiful example of what a family can do if they wish.

(Footnotes for this story can be found on p. 330)

Emily was anxious and fearful. She squirmed in her school desk; and her forehead was beading up with sweat. She was afraid of the school bully, Duke. How could she teach someone who was so hard to get along with about unity?

She had observed him every day since school had started six weeks ago. He had power. He knew how to get other kids on his side. His friends were ready to step in and defend him when he started picking on someone. If only she had power, she could teach them all. But every time she approached him and tried to tell him what she thought, she would get tongue-tied and her voice would fail her. She was afraid that Duke and his friends might beat her up, too.

She noticed that sometimes he would yell irrationally. She was afraid to even be in the same room with him then. She didn't want to feel afraid and powerless, but she did. She wanted to run home where she could feel safe. "If only I was bigger. If only I had power, I could conquer this calamity. Didn't Bahá'u'lláh say, "My calamity is My providence, outwardly it is fire and vengeance, but inwardly it is light and mercy.""?[i]

Sometimes she got Duke's kind of vengeance mixed up with how God worked. That's because her imagination was being stimulated by her fear; and she was becoming irrational, too. She was turning Duke into an ogre, a monster in her own mind. Wasn't he just a human being like her, with feelings and hopes and dreams?

Dad had told her last night that some people believed that God was vengeful, too. Emily had a loving father. She wanted to think that God was a loving father. She didn't want God to punish Duke; but it was hard to think merciful thoughts toward him when he was so mean to other kids. She said a short prayer: "Is there any Remover of difficulties save God? Say: Praised be God! He is God! All are His servants, and all abide by His bidding!"[ii] No, Duke is not a vengeful monster. He is a servant of a merciful God, and 'Abdu'l-Bahá said that we should love people, never asking whether they deserved to be loved," she decided.

Duke's bullying wasn't the only problem she saw at her school. Some of the kids were racist and used the "n" word. She hated that. It was against all that she was taught as a child in her Bahá'í family. And there were kids dealing drugs at school, too. She knew they couldn't "just say no." In her heart she knew it was more complicated than that. Her mom and dad were teaching about the equality of men and women at home. She was glad her dad seemed more tender and sensitive than the fathers of some of her friends; but at school guys and even teachers seemed very sexist. Some girls even seemed to like it that way.

There were Moslem students at school now, and other students looked down on them because they were different. So religious prejudice was also a problem. Why did so many students act so superior? Why couldn't they understand that there were many beautiful cultures and religions? She had met one Moslem student and really liked him. She was also glad that her religion, the Bahá'í Faith, stressed the importance of the elimination of religious prejudice. No wonder Bahá'u'lláh's greatest desire for the world is unity! All of the world's problems were related to unity.

On her way home from school she took a different route so she wouldn't have to pass by

Duke's house. If she walked straight home, it was only 5 blocks. The long way home was 14 blocks; but it was an interesting walk. The leaves were falling off the trees now and had turned to beautiful reds, golds, and browns. As she walked, Emily thought of the noontime prayer: "I bear witness, O my God, that Thou hast created me to know Thee and to worship Thee. I testify, at his moment, to my powerlessness and to Thy might." Then she thought: "I sure feel powerlessness over all these problems."

She was about to cross the street and take the last lap home when she turned her head suddenly to the store on her left. It was an antique store. She had always wanted to stop and look at all the treasures inside. "Why not today?" she asked herself. She pressed her face against the window. Just inside the glass was an old lamp with stained glass fragments forming a pattern on the shade. There was an antique doll with blue eyes to match her blue dress. The doll was propped against a piece of plywood that divided the display from the desk in the front room of the store.

A set of old dishes was artfully displayed, along with a few old books, an antique tractor, plus—what was that stained and tarnished thing? A cup? A goblet? It had a stem with a kind of platform at the bottom, which gave it stability. She kind of liked it. It reminded her of something. She went inside, where a woman at the counter was knitting.

"How much is that goblet in the window?" she asked.

"What grade are you in, child?" the woman asked.

"Ninth grade," Emily answered.

"Well, for your information, that goblet is a chalice—a chalice fit for a crusade."

"Wow! I'm studying about the Crusades right now in school. How much does the chalice cost?" Emily asked timidly.

"Three dollars," the woman said.

"I would like to buy it," Emily told her.

"I think I have a second one around here somewhere. I'll sell you the two of them for $5.00. Might as well have a matched set if you're going to start collecting antiques."

Emily became very excited. Not one chalice, but two! She could bring them to school and show them when she gave her report about the Crusades and the Holy Land.

The woman reached into the window display and picked up the chalice. It was dusty and had something dried and crusted on its metal surface. She blew on it and a cloud of dust exploded around her face and the chalice in her hand. She coughed a bit and turned her head.

"Where do you think the second one might be?" Emily asked.

"Try that yellow barrel over in the corner by that horsehair baby buggy," the woman suggested.

Emily looked at the large wheels of the baby buggy, which were covered with spider webs. "Ugh," she said and stepped back.

The woman urged her, "Just go around the baby buggy. A few spider webs won't hurt you."

Timidly Emily skirted the spider webs and approached the yellow barrel. It stood four feet off the ground and was piled high with stuffed animals and curtains and toy soldiers. She began to dig through them. "Do you mind if I put these things on the floor while I dig in here?" she asked.

"Go ahead. Just don't break anything. If you break it, you buy it," the old woman said and turned back to her knitting.

A stuffed bear, a clown, an elephant, a wild-eyed puppy dog, a pair of yellow curtains, a regiment of soldiers, more stuffed animals, a pair of riding pants—jodhpurs, they were called—and there, at the bottom of the yellow barrel, was the second chalice, also stained and crusted with dried matter. Emily had to tip the barrel on its side and crawl halfway in to get the chalice. She then stood the barrel back up and carefully replaced the contents.

Walking back to the counter in the front of the store, she dug into her pants pocket and found a five-dollar bill.

The woman carefully wrapped the two goblets in newspaper and placed them into a plastic grocery bag that had two handles. "Here you go, young lady," she said as she handed the bag over to Emily who gave her the five-dollar bill. "Thank you, and come again," the woman said as she put the money away.

Emily's face was beaming as she left the store and walked the last few blocks to her home. "What a find!" she said as she turned the key and opened the door. "Hi, Mom, I'm home!"

No answer. A note on the kitchen table said: "Your supper is wrapped up on the second shelf of the refrigerator. Warm it in the microwave. There's an important meeting tonight at 5. Dad and I will be home at 7. Call Grandma if you have a problem."

Emily dropped her school bag on the kitchen chair and carried the grocery bag to the kitchen sink. Opening the newspaper bundle, she slid the first chalice into the sink. Then she opened the second package. She filled the sink with hot water and added some dish soap. She washed both of the metal goblets, scrubbing the crusted matter away.

It took her about 15 minutes to do both goblets. She laid them on a towel on the counter and dried them off. They could use a little polish, she thought. She opened the door below the sink and took out the silver polish and a polishing cloth, then carried it all to her bedroom.

She sat on the edge of her bed and began to polish the first chalice. It was ornately engraved with a floral design around the rim, and on one side, presumably the front side, there was more engraving. What did it say? She rubbed it energetically with the polishing cloth and then looked at it closely. She made out the letter "P", then an "O". What was the next letter? She rubbed again with the cloth, applying more silver polish. Why the next letter was a "W".

The word was "power," she was sure of it. A little more elbow grease and the word "power" appeared. She turned to the other chalice and began polishing it with excitement. Was it a matched set? Would it say "power", too, she wondered?

No, it didn't say "power". The word was too long. But wait, yes, it *did* say "power". She rubbed it as hard as she could. It said: "powerlessness".

Imagine that! One chalice said "power" and the other "powerlessness."

Emily stood them next to each other. The base platform of the one on the left had a "V" that protruded out from it. The chalice on the right had an open notch that the "V" could slip right into. She lined up the two platforms; and as she pushed them together, they locked into place

As soon as the Chalice of Power and the Chalice of Powerlessness were locked as one, the phone rang. Emily reached to answer. "Hello," she said.

"Hi, Emmy. This is Grandma. I knew your mom and dad were gone, so I thought I'd check on you."

"Oh, hi, Grandma. Thanks for calling. Grandma, I found something exciting at the antique store—two metal chalices that lock together. One says power, and the other says powerlessness," Emily told her with great excitement. "I wonder what they are for?"

"That does sound exciting. And it's just in time for your 15th birthday," said Grandma. "I'll be right over. See you in a few minutes."

They each hung up and Emily turned back to the chalices. They were a mystery to her. She decided to go back to the kitchen and clean up the mess she had made while cleaning them. How, she wondered, were they connected to her 15th birthday, which was Saturday—tomorrow?

After she finished cleaning up the kitchen, she found her supper in the refrigerator and warmed it in the microwave. While she was eating, the doorbell rang and she ran to let her Grandma in.

"Grandma, I'm so glad to see you! How have you been? And what have you been doing lately?"

"I've been working on a special surprise for your birthday. Now, let's see those chalices that you found. They intrigue me."

"Look, Grandma, one says power and the other says powerlessness," Emily held the twin chalices up in front of her.

Her Grandmother reached for the chalices and examined them in detail.

"Grandma, I'm having a problem at school right now. There's this bully named Duke. It seems like he's got so much power. I feel intimidated by him, and so do most of the other kids at school. I wish I knew what to do, but I feel so powerless and confused," Emily confessed.

Grandma hugged her and said, "Most of us feel confused about power and powerlessness, Emmy, because they are a paradox."

"Isn't a paradox something that is contradictory, while also being true? I think that's what my teacher told us," Emily said.

"Yes, Bahá'u'lláh wants us to recognize our powerlessness, yet understand that we have great power," said Grandma.

"That does sound contradictory!" exclaimed Emily. They both heard the garage door opening up. "Oh, Mom and Dad are home!"

The kitchen door that led to the garage opened and in came Emily's mom and dad, both carrying their brief cases.

Mom set hers down on the kitchen table and the chalices caught her eye. "What's this?" she asked.

"Mom, aren't they neat? I found them at the antique store on the way home," replied Emily.

Dad turned to look at the chalices. "Power and powerlessness," he said. "That's a real find, Emmy! It's something to spark the imagination! And just in time for your birthday, too."

"Both you and Grandma have tied this to my birthday. But I don't see the relationship. Do you three have a secret that you haven't shared with me?" asked Emily.

Mom and Dad grinned. "Yes, we do, but it will have to wait for your birthday party tomorrow," answered Mom.

"Is it a present?" Emily was fairly dancing around the kitchen.

"Yes, it's the most wonderful present any parent could give a daughter when she approaches the age of maturity, and we're delighted to do so," said Dad.

"For now, why don't you start your homework? Dad and I want to eat supper; and Grandma can help us plan for tomorrow," instructed Mom.

Emily picked up the two chalices and her school bag and went to her room. She placed the chalices on the top of her dresser, sat down on her bed and opened her school bag.

Thoughts of tomorrow's birthday events kept intruding on her consciousness, but soon she was able to tune them out and settle into her studies. She studied till close to 10:30 and suddenly became aware that she was too tired to continue.

She called down the hallway. "Mom? Dad? I'm going to bed. See you in the morning."

"OK, Emmy, sleep well," called Mom.

"Is Grandma still here?"

"Yes, I am, Emmy."

"Good night, Grandma."

"Goodnight, dear. See you tomorrow at your party."

Emily brushed her teeth, washed the makeup off her face, and changed

into her pajamas. Then she lay down on her bed and snuggled into her pillow. She blinked her eyes. Something was missing. Her nightly prayers!

She got up and found her copy of *The Hidden Words* of Bahá'u'lláh and

her prayer book on her bookcase. She began to recite aloud, "O BEFRIENDED STRANGER! The candle of thine heart is lighted by the hand of My power, quench it not with the contrary winds of self and passion. The healer of all thine ills is remembrance of me, forget it not. Make My love thy treasure and cherish it even as thy very sight and life."[iii] That was from the Persian section of the Hidden Words.

She searched through the Arabic section toward the front of the book for something that seemed appropriate for the present moment. She began to recite, "O SON OF MAN! Wert thou to speed through the immensity of space and traverse the expanse of heaven, yet thou wouldst find no rest save in submission to our command and humbleness before Our Face."[iv]

"Hmm," she mused. "The first one talked about God's power, and the second one refers to our submission to His command. At least I can understand that much of power and powerlessness."

She said a prayer, turned out the light. With her nightlight on, she could make out the shape of the chalices on her dresser. She closed her eyes and went to sleep.

"Good morning, birthday girl!" her mother said when Emily came down the hallway to the kitchen the next morning.

"Good morning, Mom."

"How does it feel to be 15?"

"Sleepy!" Emily yawned.

Mom laughed. She was reviewing the "to-do" list that had to be completed before the party started at 1 p.m.

Emily and her mom spent the morning checking off each category on the list. Then, around noon, Dad arrived with the birthday cake, 30 roses^v from the florist. and take-out food so they could eat a quick lunch.

Soon guests began to arrive. It seemed like the whole Bahá'í community was there: all her friends from the Junior Youth Group, a few friends from school, Grandma and Grandpa, plus her aunts and uncles and cousins. Even her favorite teacher was there. Emily really felt special now. Presents were piling up on the buffet, but somehow she was more curious about the special surprise Mom and Dad and Grandma had been hinting about last night.

As soon as everyone was packed into the living room and a chair was found for every guest, Mom and Dad called Emily up to the chair at the front of the crowd. Grandma seemed to be beaming with pride, as she watched.

Mom had placed the two chalices of power and powerlessness on a small table at the front of the room, also right in front of Emily's chair. Dad had trimmed off the long stems of the roses and placed the 30 flowers, now about 10 inches long, on the table next to the chalice of power and powerlessness. Emily looked down and saw that there was juice in each chalice.

Her father spoke first, "Thank you, everyone, for gathering with us for this very sacred occasion. As you know, today our daughter, Emily has reached the age of 15, which is the beginning of maturity. What she doesn't know is that her mother and Grandmother and I have prepared a very important ceremony to assist her in becoming an adult."

He turned toward her and asked, "Emily, do you remember our discussion last week regarding man as the supreme Talisman?"

Emily nodded. "I remember that you told me a talisman was an object with power to protect you from evil or bring good fortune to you."

"Good memory! I began thinking about the connection of power to the word 'talisman', and I asked myself, if mankind has power, what would those powers be? I also asked myself, if Bahá'u'lláh told us in the noontime prayer that we were powerless, why would he then in His book, *Gleanings*, assure us that we had great power? Your Grandmother is now going to read a passage from *Gleanings from the Writings of Bahá'u'lláh*."

Grandma began to read: "Man is the supreme Talisman. Lack of a proper education hath, however, deprived him of that which he doth inherently possess."[vi]

Dad thanked Grandma, then said, "Now, it seems to me that when a child is born to a set of parents that his or her mother and father have three major tasks that they have to achieve. 1) They have to educate their child about God; 2) they have to educate their child about his or her inherent powers; and 3) they must also, as the child becomes capable, responsible, and cooperative, help transfer those powers in measured increments to the ownership of the child. In this way, when the child approaches the age of maturity, he or she will be able to define those powers, know what they are, and how to use them.

The youth must also know which powers they are strongest in, and know which powers need to be strengthened. Now, this process of the transfer of ownership is not something that is bestowed precisely at the age of 15, but should have been done little by little throughout childhood."

"If someone indeed has power, as Bahá'u'lláh says, then that person has authority over that power, defined as authority of self.[vii] This leads us to five important points: 1) We have to accept personal responsibility for authority of self, accepting ourselves as the ultimate decision maker for that authority; 2) we have to recognize that we are prone to making mistakes, knowing that we are not infallible.; 3) we have to recognize a source of authority higher than ourselves; 4) we have to understand the requirements of that higher authority; and 5) we have to exercise judgment in carrying out these requirements."[viii]

"Dad, then what you are saying is that when I attain the age of responsibility and you transfer some of this power to me, I must bring myself to account when I use my powers, and that if I recognize Bahá'u'lláh as the ultimate authority, then I have to know what He requires of me?" Emily asked.

"Exactly, Emily! And he tells us what is required of us in His Revelation. That's why He wants us to deepen in His Writings on a daily basis."

"But all this time I thought God wanted us to be powerless. I thought we couldn't use power at all."

"A lot of people think that, Emily. That's why your mother and I have created this ceremony. In a minute, we're going to demonstrate the differences between power and powerlessness. But first, your mom is going to give you two definitions of power."

"It's my turn now, Emmy! The first definition of power is related to "force", which is possession of control or command over others. We think of war and powerful armies, dictators, institutions, rulers and governments. But there is another more precise definition that is being used as we shift from one model or male-dominated paradigm to a more just society and that is: "effectiveness: the ability or capacity to act or perform effectively. This broader concept of power includes the capacity (the role) and the ability (the competence) to get things done by either influencing others or having access to resources. It also includes the idea of granting more autonomy to those with less power."[ix]

"So you're saying all power isn't bad, it's just how you use it and what you use it for?" asked Emily.

"Right, Emily! If you had power right now, what would you use it for?" asked her mother.

"I would use it to bring unity to the world and to cause an end to irrational behavior so people will be safe. I'm trying to solve a problem at school that I have felt powerless over for a long time. Someone there has a lot of power and he's using it in a really bad way."

"Well, let's look at power right now. Your dad and I are going to demonstrate the differences between power and powerlessness for you and all of our friends."

"Now here in front of me I have two goblets," said Dad. "One has 'power 'engraved on it, and the other says 'powerlessness'. I'm going to drink some juice from the one that has the word power on it; and I'm going to act out the different variations of power for you."

Emily's father disconnected the Chalice of Power from the Chalice of Powerlessness, and lifted the cup of power to his lips and drank. "I feel a surge of power through my mind and through every cell of my body. I feel so strong.

"I feel confident that I can accomplish whatever I want to do, through working diligently, through gaining knowledge, through developing myself. I want to be sincere. I want to be obedient to the Covenant of God. I want to assist the Cause of Bahá'u'lláh through action and prayers. I want to care for the stranger, I want to be a manifestation of the love of God. I want to walk the snow-white path."

He paused and took another long drink. "Now I want to dominate in every situation. I have expectations and I want them to be met by others. Now I've forgotten Bahá'u'lláh, and I'm taking another sip. It feels so good. I want to win—at games, at life, in relationships."

He took a fourth sip. "I want to control and fix irrational people so I don't feel anxious in their presence. I want to control their behavior and their feelings without them knowing about it."

He held the cup of power to his lips again and drank. "I want to change everyone, make them be who I want them to be so I'll feel safe." He took another drink. "I could manipulate people. They wouldn't even know it. I could be all-powerful. I could make my boss give me enough money so I could move into a mansion."

Emily's father started scowling. "No one can ever hurt me again. Nothing and no one in the whole world. No calamity!" He took another drink, and another. He was drunk with power and passion now; and he acted like surge after surge of uncontrollable energy was pulsating through his body. Friends and family were laughing at this graphic demonstration of power gone wild.

Suddenly he began shaking because he was filled with anxiety.

Someone could take his power away from him! He looked for a place to hide the Chalice of Power. He ran frantically from one corner of the dining room to another.

"It's obvious now that I have become irrational and extreme," he said. "The more I drink from the Chalice of Power, the longer this state will continue. The greater my power, the greater my fear.

Every sip of power must be tempered with meekness and humility, Emily. If you were in this position, what would you want to do?"

"I think I would want to quiet my fear and anxiety and to shelter myself from the irrational and the extreme," she answered.

"But they are within you," her father replied.

"I don't want any part of them!" she said.

"But the irrational and the extreme teach you about the balance of power and powerlessness. If I deprive you of them, you will also be deprived of the powers of the supreme Talisman."

She asked her father, "How can you say man has power when young people take drugs at school every day; there is terrible racism in the world; there is inequality between men and women, and religious prejudice is so bad that people are killing each other all around the world?"

"Man has great power despite his foibles, Emily—believe it! He is the supreme Talisman because, 'Before all else, God created the mind',[x] her father replied. "And, (Baha'u'llah revealed) 'God has endowed the essence of man, the soul of man, with the rational faculty, another word for power. All of man's powers and physical senses owe their existence to the rational faculty'."[xi]

"Then, if the essence of man is his rational faculty, why is man irrational? I really want to know. I thought if I had enough power, I could make people work together in unity," Emily said thoughtfully.

"Men and women are irrational because they don't use their powers for unity; they use them for defense. If they used them for unity, they would rid the world of all the problems you are concerned about. Man has always had some power, and used it not only for creating the great renaissance of the past, but for force and war. But it is only in Bahá'u'lláh's dispensation, for example, that woman could really begin to use her powers, because formerly she was taught to blindly obey the authority of man. She now has permission from God to have and use all of her powers. Now woman's powers have been articulated by a Messenger of God who says they can no longer be used for war, but for the development of an ever-advancing civilization. With a proper education, the supreme Talisman will be able to channel everyone's powers properly, as resources for all the world's peoples."

"But how do the irrational and the extreme teach me about the balance of power and powerlessness? That seems dumb," said Emily.

"Emily, you have a power of discernment that helps you know right from wrong. It was developed as you saw contrasts and distinctions between dark and light, truth and falsehood. The irrational and the extreme are markers, red flags, internal alarms that help you discriminate between ignorance, fantasy, falsehood, superstition, blind imitation and truth.

They help guide you away from separation and defense and toward unity.

"But there is also a paradox here. It is also the purpose of unity to move toward the irrational and the extreme even if one becomes unpopular and risks being ostracized. With unity in your heart, you sacrifice your own irrational feelings and thoughts to open the door to a potential solution. The principle of unity is the key to detaching from your own irrationality or fantasies," explained her father.

"Well, I remember when you had drunk too much from the Chalice of Power, you certainly became irrational. You were not detached in any way," Emily said.

"That experience illustrated discernment. You learned that power alone cannot be the solution to problems. Man has been trying that unsuccessfully for centuries. You will develop the power of discernment all throughout your lifetime as long as you continue to read about unity in the Writings of Bahá'u'lláh. The concept of unity will always be the touchstone for the power of discernment."

Emily looked puzzled, "What is a touchstone?"

"That which tests the genuineness or value of anything," her mother answered.

"I'm sorry, but I can't see any value in irrationality in myself or others, even if it is necessary to developing discernment," Emily countered.

Her mother touched her gently on the shoulder. "If you honor and are compassionate with the irrational and the extreme within yourself, you can become more tolerant and understanding of the irrational and the extreme within others. The irrational represents a loss of the internal purpose of the trust of God within your identity. The extreme represents the misguided force of rebellion you think is necessary to hold onto whatever small amount of identity of which you are conscious. If you despise the irrational and the extreme, you are in danger of turning away from the weak, the poor, the lost and the deprived, whom God leads plodding on their way. The quest should not be away from the irrational and the extreme, but toward them for understanding. The quest should be toward greater meekness, humility, and virtue in the face of the irrational and the extreme. The quest should be to expose and reveal the ignorance that causes the irrational and the extreme. Now, let's look at a demonstration of powerlessness."

Emily's mother lifted the chalice of powerlessness to her lips and drank. "I'm feeling less power now. I'm feeling less fear, too." She took another sip. She began to float into a powerless state around the room, and the guests began to giggle. She pretended she was floating into a calamity. "I don't have to control irrational people anymore. I don't have to try to fix them. I can allow them time to change themselves and for God to change them. I can choose meekness in affliction and humility in abasement and still feel good about myself and others."

She took another long drink. "I testify to my powerlessness and God's might."

"What is your intention?" asked Dad.

"My intention is to remember that I want to follow the commandments of Baha'u'llah, committing to obedience to a knowledge that is greater than my own. And to strive towards unity." She took another drink from the chalice of powerlessness, and another. Suddenly she said something that Emily never expected to hear from her mother!!

"I don't have any intention anymore," Mom responded. "Your intention is my intention. I have no power. I feel passive. I feel apathetic. I feel lethargic. You can make me do anything you want me to. You can choose for me, think for me, see for me, hear for me, and speak for me because I am powerless," Emily's mother said helplessly.

"Now I know that I cannot stand up alone under calamity because I am dependent and powerless. I am going to isolate myself from everything that might harm me. I'm going to stop taking risks. There is no such thing as a healthy challenge. I'm going to give up. Why should I try anymore? I have no faith in God or myself. I am a powerless victim. I have no permission to change my life. Tell me what to do. I will obey anything you say," she said, sounding very afraid.

"What is your internal intention?" her husband prodded.

"Separation, defense, and blind obedience to preserve myself from calamity and tribulation at any cost," she said.

"Emily, the perception of calamity as something bad is a reflection of the irrational within you," said her father. "Bahá'u'lláh said, 'My calamity is My providence, outwardly it is fire and vengeance, but inwardly it is light and mercy.'[xii] Emily, you cannot get true power from the Chalice of Power or abdicate power in blind obedience to others as a means of protecting yourself. We want this to be a graphic example for you, one you'll always remember—a metaphor of the concept of power. Mankind is the supreme Talisman and as such, God has given you permission to use authority of self, permission to use your powers with wisdom and discernment to protect yourself and to help yourself grow."

"But how do I develop these powers?" Emily asked.

"That's the next part of our ceremony. Your mother and I are going to bestow these powers upon you one-by-one right now." Emily's father wiped out the empty chalices with a napkin and her mother brought a stack of cards to the table. Father filled each chalice with water. Grandma laid 30 roses on the table beside them.

Her mother spoke. "Emily, though there are 30 roses here to represent 30 powers, your father and I want you to know that there are many more powers than this that you have access to. Every Name of God is a power and in the Long Healing Prayer, there are 126 names of God. If you consider all the different virtues, each of them is a power. Bahá'u'lláh and 'Abdu'l-Bahá used the words virtue, capacity, force, faculty, ability, gift, tool, and capability interchangeably with the word power. So, let's begin. Here's the first sheet we want you to read aloud. Your dad and I will alternate the parent readings."

EMILY'S COMING OF AGE CEREMONY

To be read by Emily:

I am a human being. To be human is to have a physical body that I can see. But part of me is invisible. That part of me that I can't see is called my soul. My body wears out, but my soul lasts forever.

I have physical or outer powers and I also have spiritual or inner powers. While I am growing up I will develop many of my outer and inner powers, that grouped together, are called "Authority of Self," a psychological term. They are also called the powers of the servant. With these powers I will discover my gifts, my internal intention, and create knowledge, art, and science, and find my place in God's plan.

Authority of self can be defined as the freedom and ability to use the mental powers that God gave to me to make rational and moral choices; with the expectation that I will regulate my emotions; granting me the right or permission to act independently with the understanding that one has personal limitations. My parents or caregivers transfer authority of self to me in small stages as I achieve the ability to be capable, responsible, and cooperative.

My Creator has given me these 30 powers and more in a universe of laws, which means that I have freedom within limitations even when I become an adult. God's laws are my limitations or boundaries, as well as His mercy to me. His Covenant reminds me of His blessings and bounties as well as my limitations.

Emily's Father:

"A Covenant in a religious sense is a binding agreement between God and man, whereby God requires of man certain behavior in return for which He guarantees certain blessings, or whereby He gives man certain bounties in return for which He takes from those who accept them an undertaking to behave in a certain way."[xiii]

Emily's Mother:
It is my hope as your parent/caregiver/guardian that you will abide by the Covenant of God in every moral or behavioral choice that you make. I now extend to you with this rose that represents the *power of thought*.

To be read by Emily:
Some of the powers of my soul, my spiritual powers, include the *power of thought*, which reflects upon reality or truth. I think about the knowledge I am learning. I plan with my thoughts. I can say what I think. I can discover many things about myself by listening to my thoughts. I can develop spiritual perceptions by exploring with my thoughts. (She places the rose in the vase.)

To be read by Emily's Mother:
We now bestow upon you the *power of discernment*. This flower represents the fact that we are transferring this power to you.

To be read by Emily:
With a fully developed *power of discernment*, I can know the difference between right and wrong, truth and fantasy, justice and injustice, wisdom and foolishness, and the many degrees between perfection and imperfection. It is through Bahá'u'lláh's Revelation that the power of discernment is developed: " ... through Whom

truth shall be distinguished from error and the wisdom of every command shall be tested."[xiv]

To be read by the parents:
We now bestow upon you the *affective power*. And with this rose so signify that your feelings are a state of consciousness through which you can gather facts that are important to your moral and behavioral choices.

To be read by Emily:

My feelings are a power, too, *the affective power*. When I am sad, I can cry. When I feel happy, I can laugh and smile. When I feel scared, I can ask for help. When I am worried, I can tell someone I trust. When I am angry, I can tell others about my feelings and work out a solution instead of acting out my anger. And although my feelings (emotions) are a guide to how I feel about certain situations, I will gather information from all of my powers to regulate my moral and behavioral choices. I will try to understand what is God's will for me rather than act on how I feel.

To be read by Emily's mother

I now affirm with this rose, as I have all of these years, that you have the right to your own *power of identity*; and that I will seek with all my power to support who you are becoming even though that may be different than my own identity.

To be read by Emily:

There are certain powers that are fundamental to the development of my *power of identity* or individual self. I am helpless to develop my identity and my gifts without the freedom to use my power of speech and my power of reasoning. If these are prohibited, my identity or individual self and my gifts, the treasures God has placed within my soul, lie dormant, unexplored, unmined for the Glory of God.

To be read by Emily's Father:
Since you were a child, I always respected your *power of choice*, which is also called the *power of volition*, and attempted to guide you into being accountable for your choices. We now, as this rose represents, grant you in greater measure the authority to make moral and behavioral choices that are in keeping with the Covenant of God. For that is the only way we know to help you be responsible for every choice that you make.

To be read by Emily:
I have the *power to choose* as I search for my good and the good of others. As I take action on my choices, new ideas will come to me to help me achieve the next active step in my search to develop my gifts. It is when I "will" myself to action—using volition—that I can make important changes in my life. If my

power of volition is blocked, I will not be able to develop my internal purpose. I will be passive and compliant instead, abdicating my power of choice to others in blind obedience. Bahá'u'lláh writes,

> "And now, concerning thy question regarding the creation of man. Know thou that all men have been created in the nature made by God, the Guardian, the Self-Subsisting. Unto each one hath been prescribed a pre-ordained measure, as decreed in God's mighty and guarded Tablets. All that which ye potentially possess can, however, be manifested only as a result of your own volition. Your own acts testify to this truth."[xv]

To be read by Emily's Mother:
This rose signifies that we are transferring the *power of speech* to you in the hopes that you will speak truth for yourself and seek justice for others with your speech.

To be read by Emily:
My voice is also a power—the *power of speech*. I have a right to speak, to tell others who I am. I can speak my truth respectfully, with passion and meekness without fear of punishment. When I speak my truth out loud, I know myself better and others get to know me, too. I can use my voice to say "no" to those who seek to harm me and set verbal boundaries with others. I can also say "yes" when I

feel safe. I can use my voice to state what I think is fair or unfair; and I can also tell others when I lose my good feelings about myself. My voice asserts, affirms, and acknowledges my feelings and my thoughts and makes my truth real to others and me. In any event, context, or relationship that is sexist, racist, or discriminatory and prejudiced, I am less likely to lose my self-worth if my *power of speech* and my *power of identity* are affirmed and supported. Shoghi Effendi encourages us with this quotation:

> "...it is not only the right but the sacred obligation of every member to express freely and openly his views, without being afraid of displeasing or alienating any of his fellow-members."[xvi]

To be read by Emily's Mother:
We have always encouraged you to ask questions, but now, at this point of your life, and with this rose, we affirm the grave importance of your seeking the mysteries of life with the power of *intellectual investigation of truth.*

To be read by Emily:
I have the power to ask questions freely—to investigate, to be curious, to examine, to experiment, to test—and thereby, to discover new things as I grow up. This is *the power of intellectual investigation of truth.* This will enable me to change my mind as I discover new knowledge and will prevent me from

imitating the traditions of the past, which may need to be changed in my life. This is a real power that is denied to many people who are deprived because they live in countries where education isn't equally extended to all. People who are forced to blindly obey are also deprived of this power. 'Abdu'l-Bahá gives us this guidance:

> "He must not be an imitator or blind follower of any soul. He must not rely implicitly upon the opinion of any man without investigation; nay, each soul must seek intelligently and independently, arriving at a real conclusion and bound only by that reality. The greatest cause of bereavement and disheartening in the world of humanity is ignorance based upon blind obedience."[xvii]

To be read by Emily's Father
With this next rose we seek to encourage you to deepen your *power of understanding*, even though your perspective and understanding is uniquely yours.

To be read by Emily:
I can seek to know and understand with the questions that I ask. This is *the power of understanding*. I can also develop a deeper understanding of truth by daring to ask questions. My understanding is a power that may be different from yours, but when I share

my unique understanding with you, we may together achieve an understanding of truth that is completely different and more enlarged. This is the purpose of consultation. Here is the importance that Bahá'u'lláh places on consultation:

> "Consultation bestoweth greater awareness and transmuteth conjecture into certitude. It is a shining light which, in a dark world, leadeth the way and guideth. For everything there is and will continue to be a station of perfection and maturity. The maturity of understanding is made through consultation."[xviii]

> "In this Day whatsoever serveth to reduce blindness and to increase vision is worthy of consideration. This vision acteth as the agent and guide for true knowledge. Indeed, in the estimation of men of wisdom keenness of understanding is due to keenness of vision."[xix]

To be read by Emily's Mother:
To pave the way for your life as an adult, I bestow upon you with this rose, the *power of memory*, which will forever serve your ability to remember consequences for your moral and behavioral choices.

To be read by Emily:

My *memory is a special power* that can help me remember what I learn whether that is information, skills, lessons, rules, plans, experiences, places, people, events, or the commandments of God. Remembering unpleasant experiences can help me change my behavior and my future. When my feelings, memory, imagination and other powers work together, they create an internal alarm that lets me know when I am in danger or that there are consequences for the behavior I am about to choose. 'Abdu'l-Bahá advises us:

> "Man has also spiritual powers: imagination, which conceives things; thought, which reflects upon realities; comprehension, which comprehends realities, memory, which retains whatever man imagines, thinks and comprehends."[xx]

To be read by Emily's Father:
The *power of imagination* can serve you artistically, creatively, as well as in problem-solving. This rose signifies that it must always be used responsibly.

To be read by Emily:
Imagination is a power that is important to the development of my gifts. I can imagine what I'm going to be when I grow up. My imagination helps me dream things into happening. Sometimes I will have to test my imagination with other powers to see if this vision is helpful or harmful. If it is helpful, I

can create something of value. If it is harmful, I will need to make responsible choices with it.

To be read by Emily's Mother:
This next rose represents a very important power, the *power of inner vision and inner hearing* through which you will listen to the sacred voice within your soul. May you always heed this call within.

To be read by Emily:
In addition to these powers, I will also develop an inner voice, inner vision, and inner ear that will help me understand and respond to that which is sacred. *My power of inner vision* is a special gift to guide me when I need to make choices about what is right or wrong. It will help me when I need to use wisdom. If these inner powers have been acknowledged instead of discounted, and if my powers of identity and choice are not withheld from me, I am less likely to be swayed by others to break the laws God has given to me for my protection. In *Some Answered Questions*, 'Abdu'l-Bahá states:

> "This is a power which encompasses all things, comprehends their realities, discovers all the hidden mysteries of beings, and through this knowledge controls them: it even perceives things which do not exist outwardly; that is to say intellectual realities which are not

sensible, and which have no outward existence, because they are invisible; so it comprehends the mind, the spirit, the qualities, the characters, the love and sorrow of man, which are intellectual realities." [32]

To be read by Emily's Father:
Perhaps the most important power to the Bahá'í youth is the *power of recognizing Him* (Bahá'u'lláh). Strengthening this power has enabled you to become a Bahá'í and will help you desire to obey His commandments. This power is also connected to your ability to recognize "truth." With this rose I create awareness and confirmation of this power.

To be read by Emily:
Another important power I have is the *power of recognizing Him*, which includes the ability to recognize truth. This is a power that dwells within each human being that enables him or her to recognize God and His Manifestations, or the Messengers of God. Bahá'u'lláh advises us:

> "The first duty prescribed by God for His servants is the recognition of Him Who is the Dayspring of His Revelation and the Fountain of His laws, Who representeth the

---

[32] 'Abdu'l- Baha, Some Answered Questions, p. 186

Godhead in both the Kingdom of His Cause and the world of creation."[xxi]

It follows, therefore, that every man hath been, and will continue to be, able of himself to appreciate the Beauty of God, the Glorified. Had he not been endowed with such a capacity, how could he be called to account for his failure?"[xxii]

To be read by Emily's Father:
As your parents/caregivers it is our hope that you will develop wisdom as you build your character and grow in maturity. To signify the *power of wisdom*, we present this rose to you.

To be read by Emily:

I am strengthened with the *power of wisdom*, which is the capacity to judge rightly in matters relating to life and conduct. When I use good judgment in making decisions, I am considered to have used wisdom. Bahá'u'lláh elaborates on this:

> "Above all else, the greatest gift and the most wondrous blessing hath ever been and will continue to be Wisdom. It is man's unfailing Protector. It aideth him and strengtheneth him. Wisdom is God's Emissary and the Revealer of His Name the Omniscient."[xxiii]

To be read by Emily's Mother:
This next rose represents a realization that even as intelligent, fully functioning, mature, and educated adults, we still have limitations and that we have a *faculty (or power) of shame* that is designed to help us correct our behavior and limit some choices.

To be read by Emily:
Because God created me to be independent, he also saw the need for me to have the *power of limitations*, giving me room within the limits to make some choices, but not all. This power helps me recognize that though I have free will, God desires that I call myself to account and regulate my own behavior. I do this because I recognize and understand that there are consequences for my behavior.

> "Every created thing will be enabled (so great is this reflecting power) to reveal the potentialities of its pre-ordained station, will recognize its capacity and limitations, and will testify to the truth that 'He, verily, is God; there is none other God besides Him.'"[xxiv]

The faculty of shame, which guards me against that which is unworthy and unseemly,[xxv] and the fear of God are also a part of the power of limitations.[xxvi]

To be read by Emily's Mother:

We are presenting you with this rose to draw your attention to the *power of perception*, which will be unique to your experience. We want you to know that there are multiple perceptions in any community and each perception belonging to another is to be treated with respect and accepted as the right of that individual. Know that perceptions can be altered during consultation

To be read by Emily:
I also have the *power of perception* that helps me interpret what I see and experience with my five senses. There is a danger that my power of perception may be influenced or clouded by negative emotions such as resentment, hate, and irrational fear; but I can make positive perceptions when I use such virtues as patience, courage, magnanimity, and compassion. When I read the sacred Writings, they help me combine the power of discernment with the power of perception, thus helping to shape the way I interpret the events of my life.

To be read by Emily's Father:
We pray that you will have the courage to use your *power of reasoning* both internally as you seek to avoid being a blind follower of tradition, as well as verbally with others in your search for truth. This rose is symbolic of your *power of reasoning*.

To be read by Emily:

I use my *power of reasoning* to evaluate my experiences and to draw conclusions from them. Discussing my thoughts and point of view, including all the facts, helps me discover reality. And most important of all, reasoning out loud helps the development of my identity. 'Abdu'l-Bahá says:

> "Know ye that God has created in man the power of reason, whereby man is enabled to investigate reality. God has not intended man to imitate blindly his fathers and ancestors. He has endowed him with mind, or the faculty of reasoning, by the exercise of which he is to investigate and discover the truth, and that which he finds real and true he must accept. He must not be an imitator or blind follower of any soul. He must not rely implicitly upon the opinion of any man without investigation."[xxvii]

To be read by Emily's Mother:
We have provided you with a stable family life so that you could develop a measure of trust in us, in others, and in yourself so that at the age of maturity your power of faith would give you the confidence to negotiate your way in the world. Please accept this rose that represents the *power of faith*.

To be read by Emily:
Throughout my life my family and the Bahá'í community will supply me with an abundance of faith experiences, which cause my *power of faith* to grow. 'Abdu'l-Bahá' tells us that faith is conscious knowledge.[33] If I am conscious of my emotions, my thoughts, and the way I am feeling physically, plus live in a nurturing family and community, I will learn to trust and have faith in myself, in others, and in God.

To be read by Emily's Father:
The *cognitive power* allows you to know God and to have self-knowledge. Through the knowledge of God, you will be enabled to develop your power of wisdom, as well, for they are connected. This rose represents your power to know God, which is the greatest glory in this human world.

To be read by Emily:
The *cognitive power is my power of knowing*. It is being able to know myself (self-awareness), using my knowledge to form judgments (the power of wisdom), to make choices, and to know God. It can include knowledge of physical sensation and mental perception. It is through the knowledge of God that I will be enabled to develop right morals.

> "... that which is the cause of everlasting life, eternal honor, universal

---

[33] Tablets of 'Abdu'l-Baha, p. 549

135

enlightenment, real salvation and prosperity is, first of all, the knowledge of God. It is known that the knowledge of God is beyond all knowledge, and it is the greatest glory of the human world. For in the existing knowledge of the reality of things there is material advantage, and through it outward civilization progresses; but the knowledge of God is the cause of spiritual progress and attraction, and through it the perception of truth, the exaltation of humanity, divine civilization, rightness of morals and illumination are obtained."[xxviii]

To be read by Emily's Mother:
It is possible to make some amazing discoveries when you search the Word of God as well as the collective knowledge of humankind, because God created within you the *power of discovery*. May this rose remind you to delight in your search and be fearless in asking questions.

To be read by Emily:
When I have arrived at new knowledge, it is because I have searched (asked questions, probed) and studied until my *power of discovery* has developed sufficiently. This is how all the sciences, arts, crafts, and inventions that were hidden secrets were discovered. In order for me to experience the power

of discovery, I have to assert my right to ask questions, which is the power of intellectual investigation of truth.

To be read by Emily's Father:
To consciously reflect is an asset that can help bring about your own well-being and inner harmony, as well as that of the community in which you serve. It is also the source of the development of the gifts that you bring to the world. May this rose encourage you to use your *power of reflection*.

To be read by Emily:
When I think or consider seriously while in a meditative, pensive state, I am using my *power of reflection*. 'Abdu'l-Bahá says that conscious reflection is a power belonging to man:

> "The source of crafts, sciences and arts is the power of reflection. Make ye every effort that out of this ideal mine there may gleam forth such pearls of wisdom and utterance as will promote the well-being and harmony of all the kindreds of the earth."[xxix]

To be read by Emily's Mother:
During your life as an adult you will have to use your *power of induction* to infer the meaning of your experiences. The greatness of Bahá'u'lláh's

Revelation is that His principles both infer solutions and act upon your will to motivate you to act with justice.

To be read by Emily:
The *power of induction* is to infer or draw a conclusion based on my observations, perceptions, emotions, memory, or inner vision. Certain principles or laws are considered "powers" that act upon my will by inducing me to act correctly. This is how Bahá'u'lláh's spiritual principles act upon the will of humankind to precipitate solutions to social problems.

To be read by Emily's Father:
Some people seem to be able to predict the future simply because they have gathered some facts and made some astute observations. You have an ability that allows you to do that, too. It's called the *power of deduction* through which you have a general situation and then reason to a particular conclusion. With this rose, we give you permission to further develop the power of deduction.

To be read by Emily:
There are times that I use my *power of deduction*. Deduction is reasoning from the general to the particular. 'Abdu'l-Bahá wrote of deduction in regard to the power of discovery, "By intellectual processes and logical deductions of reason this superpower in

man can penetrate the mysteries of the future and anticipate its happenings."[xxx]

To be read by Emily's Mother:
A power that will help you relate to other children of God is the *power of receptivity* through which you can take in their reality. This rose reminds you to stay free of prejudice and doubt that can block this power.

To be read by the Emily:
I have the *power of receptivity*, as well. This means that I am capable of taking in or receiving the knowledge of God and the reality of other human beings. I can be receptive to joy and peace and I can also be receptive to negative emotions. There are certain things that block this power such as an extreme attachment to my cultural heritage, prejudice, cynicism, doubt, and whatever role I am expected to play in life as a male or female.

To be read by Emily's Father:
We can best answer God's call to service through action. This rose represents the *power of response* that not only renews your soul, but also helps to move the Cause of God forward. May you always remember to answer God through action.

To be read by Emily:
The *power of response* is a power that "answers" God, authority or the requirements of life, maturity or

love, through physical, emotional, or mental action to a stimulus, influence, or principle that has been received. The Universal House of Justice, calls it the power of execution and the power of action. When my response is one of joy, acceptance, or mercy, it becomes a renewal of the soul. When my response is cruelty, vengeance, or alienation, it causes remoteness from God. If I am responseless, I give no reply, no answer to the reality of another who may be longing for a response. The power of response is the capacity to fulfill a trust, a need, or obligation.

To be read by Emily's Mother:
At other times you will have to remain inactive while you are waiting for something important to happen. You will also need to have faith as you anticipate a future good. This is the *power of anticipation,* of which this rose is symbolic.

To be read by Emily:
There is a power through which I express expectations that is called the *power of anticipation.* Bahá'u'lláh leads us in developing this power in the opening to the long obligatory prayer in which he tells us to mentally and spiritually *await* the mercy and presence of our Lord. The Bible expresses it with these phrases: "waiting on the Lord" or "resting in God". And, "I truly believe I will live to see the Lord's goodness. Wait for the Lord's help. Be strong and brave, and wait for the Lord's help."[xxxi] To wait is to remain inactive until

something anticipated happens. Waiting on the Lord and trusting in God, having an expectation or anticipation of good, are also elements of the power of faith.

To be read by the Emily's Father:
Staying alert and attentive to the needs of others as well as yourself involves the *power of attention*, which will assist you in teaching the Cause of God as well as being obedient to a higher authority. We give you this rose then to represent this power.

To be read by Emily:
Being a good student becomes easier when I use my *power of attention*. This is a power of applying my mind and observant powers to the tasks of learning lessons or serving God or my parents. It is a state of being alert to every aspect of each situation I face, whether it is teaching the cause, helping a person in need, or being obedient to an authoritative summons. All the while learning humbly what is expected of me, remaining ever open or receptive to discover a possible action in response to what is required of me.

To be read by Emily's Mother:
The *power of accountability* is a power that corrects your conscience and your character. It needs to be used on a daily basis as you review the things you have done or left undone. It can protect your boundaries and the boundaries of others with which you have

relationships.   Take time to see if you need
repentance and/or forgiveness. Remembering that
you have limitations is an assist to bringing yourself
to account.

To be read by Emily:
The *power of accountability* is a power I would use
every day to bring myself to account, to straighten
my path, using the powers of discernment, memory,
reflection, and receptivity to the Word of God to
determine if I need to repent and seek forgiveness,
to change my character or conscience. "O SON OF
BEING! Bring thyself to account each day ere thou
art summoned to a reckoning.   For death;
unheralded, shall come upon thee and thou shalt be
called to give account for thy deeds."

To be read by Emily:
These are some of my powers then: intellectual
investigation of truth, perception, feelings, wisdom,
discernment, thinking, understanding, memory,
identity, imagination, inner vision, speech, volition or
will, the power to recognize Him or truth,
limitations, reasoning, faith, knowing, discovery,
reflection, induction, deduction, anticipation,
receptivity, response and attention, and the power of
accountability. With these powers I can make
decisions that are in keeping with the Covenant of
Bahá'u'lláh and create a life that will bring me
stability and tranquility.

Because I have the right to dignity and good feelings about myself, my right to make decisions and choices can never be taken from me unless I am harming myself or others.

While I am growing up, I will learn to respect and obey the just authority of my parents, my teachers, and the principal of my school, as well as my future employer. I will also learn to obey the authority of God as found in His Revelation. As I read the sacred Writings of Bahá'u'lláh, I will learn that there will always be sacred boundaries beyond which I cannot go and within which I can choose responsible freedom.

If I make a choice that I am uncomfortable with, I can change it. Developing responsibility for my choices helps me to feel good about myself. I will work on developing the powers of authority of self so I can have a strong inner self. I have a great responsibility to not hurt anyone with these powers. And I will learn that my powers become stronger when used in service to God and humanity as well as unity and cooperation with others.

To be read by Emily's Mother:
You will need to choose to develop these powers by reading the Word of God, and then use them to create unity with others and to develop an ever-advancing civilization. When you develop the powers of the supreme Talisman with humility and obedience to God, 'Abdu'l-Bahá says you will gain

faith 'as steadfast as a rock that no storms can move. … As ye have faith, so shall your powers and blessings be.'"[xxxii] Faith is a balance of power and powerlessness; a concept or principle that only works in obedience to the commandments of God."

Then, when the swords flash in calamity, you will be able to go forward in meekness. And when the shafts fly in tribulation, you will be able to press onward in humility, using your powers as a resource to benefit humankind instead of as force. Ya'Bahá'u'l'Abhá!

"Dad?" Emily said after a few moments of silence.

"Yes, Emily?"

"I'm not afraid of the bully at school anymore. He really doesn't have any power, does he?"

"No, Emily. He's powerless," answered her father.

"Thanks, Mom and Dad. And thank you, too, Grandma!"

"You're welcome, Emily."

"Happy Birthday!" everyone cheered.

Chapter Four

THE GIRL AND BOY WHO

WERE JOINED AT THE

HEART

The baby girl was 13 months old when she first saw her 15 month old baby-boy friend. She toddled over to him and threw her arms around him so fast and so tightly that they both tumbled to the ground. Baby girl said, "Boy!" Baby boy said, "Girl!" And then he kissed her cheek. At that moment they were joined at the heart.

Whenever she cried, he rushed to her side. Whenever he fell down, she ran to help him get up. They both loved red. They both loved stuffed animals. They both loved ice cream. And she loved him and he loved her. And their heart went a happy bump-bump, bump-bump, bump-bump.

Then one day her Mommy told her she had to wear pink because she was a girl. And his Mommy told him he had to wear blue because he was a boy. They were both unhappy because they both loved red, and their heart went a sad ping-ping instead of a happy bump-bump, bump-bump.

Then the next month her Mommy saw her playing with her stuffed animal and told her that she had to play with a girl doll. And his Mommy told him he had to play with a fire engine. After all, she was a girl and he was a boy, and this is the way things were. And he liked her doll, and she liked his fire engine but the Mommy's said they couldn't trade. And their heart went a sad ping-ping instead of a happy bump-bump.

Then when he was two years old and she was almost catching up with him, her Mommy took her to a bridal shop and said, "OOOOOh, look baby girl, pretty bride dress. Isn't it beautiful?" Her Mommy told baby girl she would wear one someday because girls eventually do that. They need someone to take care of them. And baby boy's Mommy took him to a fire station and showed him the fire truck and said, "Baby boy, someday you will drive a fire truck like this. All boys eventually do that because boys are very brave.

And baby girl giggled when she looked at the beautiful bride dress, and baby boy giggled when he looked at the fire truck. Baby boy was proud that he was called brave. He stuck out his chest and asked for a sword so he could show the world how brave he was. But when the neighbor's dog barked at him through the fence, he ran inside real fast pretending he wanted a cookie. And baby girl liked being taken care of so she smiled about the beautiful bride dress. She knew she was loved. Someone had to take care

of her because she was too little; and she went to
sleep dreaming about the beautiful bride dress. But
their heart went a sad ping-ping instead of a happy
bump-bump.

Also, when they were two years old, their
Mommies and Daddies had to discipline them so
they wouldn't get into trouble, so they told them
"no" 432 times a day and told them "yes", giving
them a positive acknowledgement only 32 times a
day.[xxxiii] And their heart went a sad ping-ping
instead of a happy bump-bump.

And when he was four years old and she was
almost catching up to him, he told her he was braver
than she was, and his daddy was brave and his
grandpa was brave and girls weren't brave. And now
that he was 4 years old, he could walk down to the
corner and she couldn't. Then she began to pull her
heart away from his. She thought she was brave, but
she couldn't prove it because no one ever let her do
anything brave. She wanted to, she tried to, but
every time she tried, someone screamed, "Get away
from there! You're going to get hurt!" So her heart
went a sad ping-ping instead of a happy bump-
bump.

And the little boy was praised for being brave,
but when he went down to the corner, there was a
bigger boy there who almost hit him with a stick;
and he was so scared that he ran all the way home.
After that when people called him brave, he didn't
believe in himself. He knew he wasn't brave and he
thought girls were lucky because they didn't have to
pretend to be brave. And his heart went a sad ping-

ping instead of a happy bump-bump, and he began to pull his heart away from hers.

When he was 7 years old, his daddy gave him a BB gun because future men had to know how to be manly and learn to hunt. His father also gave him a Lego set so he could learn how to construct things and develop his mind. Her Mommy made her sleep in these awful, hard pins to curl her hair, because future brides had to learn how to be pretty. For her birthday she was given a kitchen set, complete with refrigerator, stove and ironing board, to play with. He was glad he didn't have to wear those ugly pins in his hair. And she didn't like the fact that he was going to hunt poor defenseless animals and shoot them dead. She also wanted a Lego set so she could build something, but that wasn't to be. And each began to pull the heart they shared further and further apart. And their heart went a sad ping-ping instead of a happy bump-bump.

When they were 12 years old, their heart was finally severed because he stood with three of his friends after school and mocked and ridiculed her as being a stupid girl. He was jealous because she was so smart and had so many gifts. Tears rolled down her cheeks because she really loved him and couldn't understand why he could hurt her so. She turned up her nose and walked away from him, deciding to pretend to be dumb from then on. From that moment on she began to discount all her gifts. What good were they? The teachers only called on boys during class anyway.

As he watched her slowly walk away from him, his secret feeling in his heart was shame. He felt shamed by her because she would no longer look at him. He also felt shame because he had discovered a gift in his heart that was a "girl" gift. And that could not be.

Now their heart no longer went ping-ping or bump-bump. And she wept because she thought one day she might have been his bride. And he wept because he thought one day he might have been her beloved groom. And now they knew that was never to be.

And then one day when she was almost 25 years old, she told someone that she was just about ready to graduate from college, but she didn't know what she was going to do when she finished. Her friend asked her what she majored in. She said, "Well, first of all I majored in English because I thought I wanted to be a teacher. But after I got into it, I just didn't know. Then I changed my major to nursing because I thought I would be a nurse. And then I didn't know if I really wanted that. So I changed to chemistry because I thought I'd become a pharmacist. Now I'm so confused that I really don't know what I want to be. But I've got this wonderful boy friend and he's got a great job. He wants me to marry him. I think what I really want to do is get married and have babies. Only I just don't know. I just don't know." Her friend couldn't detect a heartbeat at all.

And when her childhood friend had turned 25 years old, someone asked him what he was going to do now that he had graduated from college. He said, "I've already had 6 job offers and I'm going to choose the best of the best. I plan to travel as much as possible and find out where life leads me. There's a great big, wonderful world out there just waiting for me!" After he said that, he hopped on his Harley, flexed his muscles and raced down the road, but in his heart of hearts he was very frightened. Strange, his friend didn't detect a heartbeat either.

About five miles down the road the child-man skidded on his motorcycle while going around a dangerous curve in the road. He hit a tree and flew 30 feet into the air. When help arrived they could not hear a heart beat. "He's dead," they said; and they covered him up with a blanket. Lying next to him was a book of poetry.

On her way home from class the child-woman saw the crowd that had formed at the curve. For some reason her heart started beating wildly. It wasn't a ping-ping. It was bump-bump, bump-bump, bump-bump. She stopped her car, got out and approached the scene of the accident. The closer she got to the man lying on the ground, the more wildly her heartbeat.

"I'm sorry, Mam. The young man is dead. You'll have to get back." "No! He's not dead! I know it!" She inched up closer to him and his hand moved. "Oh, my God! He moved. Did you see that?" said one paramedic to another. She dropped down to her childhood friend, uncovered his face, and held his hand. He opened his eyes and gazed into hers. His heart was beating wildly. Together they said, "I....I...I've missed you!" Then he said, "I'm not the brave person I was pretending to be." She looked at him with the softest eyes and said, "You don't have to be brave and you don't have to be strong all the time. You can just be yourself."

"And you don't have to pretend you are dumb," he said. "It's important to develop your gifts and take pride in your achievements. I'm sorry I discounted them. I've been discounting my own gifts, too. You see, I like to write poetry." "You do? I didn't know that! I love poetry! That's wonderful!" she offered.

"Hey, guy? Are you all right? We couldn't get a heart beat a while ago and we thought you were gone." "Yeah, I'm all right – now!" And after filling out a report, they walked to her car. Their hearts were joined together again, beating as one – bump-bump, bump-bump, bump-bump. This time only her car went ping-ping, and he said, "We're going to have to get that fixed."

Questions:

1. What is your favorite color? Make a listing of all of the colors of your clothes in your closet and in your drawer. Are there one or two colors that are usually assigned to girls, like pink, yellow, or pastel green?

2. Do you have "toys" that are usually assigned to girls, like dolls instead of Legos?
   What kinds of toys, crafts, or projects do you dream about doing? Is there something you would want to invent?

3. Are you already wearing make-up, nylons and high-heels and reading fashion magazines that tell girls how to be more beautiful or attractive? What do you like about yourself? What are your best qualities? Do you excel in patience? Do you strive toward justice? In what ways?

4. What do boys do that you would like to do? What are the careers that are usually assigned to men that you would like to engage in? Name some famous men and women who have broken through the stereotypes and have careers that have broken down the barriers.

5. Baha'u'llah and the Bab prayed that the slaves would be freed. They also taught us that women will be emancipated, which means that they would also be freed. What do you think that would mean for women in today's world?

6. Statistics prove that boys are called on in school more than girls and encouraged more to study math and science. How could you work toward greater equality between the sexes in school?

7. In what way do you see teachers making prejudiced assumptions about girls abilities and gifts in school? How could this be corrected? Are there "girl" gifts and "boy" gifts?

8. 'Abdu'l-Baha and Baha'u'llah state that women will enter the same kinds of activities as men even though they will have the responsibility of raising children and being mothers. What will men need to do in order to help women do both?

9. Do you think you would be a good manager, boss, or supervisor when you get a job as an

adult? How would you assist women in attaining greater equality in the workplace?

10. The story "The Girl and Boy Who Were Joined at the Heart" is about prejudice and stereotyping of girls, teaching them to be less than boys. What does equality look like to you? What does inequality feel like? What would make you feel more equal in your family, in your school, and in your Baha'i community?

11: How do stereotyping and rigid roles hurt boys and men?

What do we do with feelings that seem out of control when we most want to maintain our dignity? How do we help our children to connect an event with the feeling that follows? Chapter Five is an examination of "The Importance of the Development of a Feeling Language in Children and Adults." As you will see, each Chapter in this manual can serve as a separate workshop.

Chapter Five

The Importance of the Development

Of a Feeling Language for Children and

Adults

Presented in Japan

The program that I have chosen today is to teach you about children's feelings. But for you to understand children's feelings, you have to understand your own feelings. You'll find a blank piece of paper in your folder. Draw a line in the middle of it from top to bottom. Write down a feeling word on the left side for what you feel right now about being so busy about coming down to this program.

(Pause and give them time to do so.)

On the right side, write down all the feeling words you can think of in 3 minutes. Don't worry, this is just for you. You won't have to show it to anyone else.

(Pause for 3 minutes to give them time to do so.)

Count the feeling words. I always take only 2 minutes for this in the US and the highest number I've ever gotten is 25. How many had 15 or more?

(Wait for show of hands.) How many had 18 or more? (Wait for show of hands.) How many had 20? (Wait for show of hands.) In order to teach children and nurture them, we need to know "feeling language" which is very difficult if it hasn't been taught or allowed. The next thing I want to do is to hand out the list of feeling words. There are over 250 words for feelings in English. Yet we have troubles expressing our feelings.

When I was a little girl, and I tried to express my feeling, my mother hit me in the mouth. And my mouth bled. My father beat me with the belt when he was angry. And I had red marks all over my legs. I could not cry. But I was hit if I was happy, too. Things were very mixed up in my family life. So I learned not to express my feelings at all. This was very confusing to me. When I grew up, all I did was rage. I raged at my sewing machine, when it didn't work right. I raged at my dog. I raged at my children and I am very ashamed of that. But the only feeling I had was rage. So I had to learn from the beginning how to express all of my feelings.
(Hand out the paper with the feeling words in English) go to www.skylarkpubl.com and click on Free Materials.
If you'd look at this piece of paper, you'll see the many feelings that there are in the English language. There are even more feeling words than that, that we don't have words for.

Here is what it sounds like to make a sentence that describes how you feel when you are upset or even when you feel happy. "I feel sad when you call me names because then I think you don't like me."

Or "I feel elated when you ask me what I think because then I know you think I am your equal."

"I feel reassured when we have an opportunity to consult because both of our view points can be discussed openly."

"I feel frightened when you bully me because I'm afraid you might hit me."

"I feel grateful when you acknowledge my contribution at work because then I know you appreciate my intelligence.

Pick out three feeling words on the list that describes how you have felt during the past week and make feeling statements about them to the person sitting next to you. They don't have to be revealing statements. They can just be everyday common feelings. Nothing private or secretive that would embarrass you.

(Give them 10 minutes to do this assignment.)
Now, I'd like to hand out another piece of paper with all the faces that show feelings. Do you recognize some of these facial expressions? Do some of them make you laugh? Have you ever seen any of these expressions on the faces of your children or friends? You don't have to fill out all the

blanks under the faces right now. It's a tool you can use with your own children.

(Hand out the paper with the faces that show feelings.)

You can point to a face and ask your child or student, "Do you recognize that feeling? What is that little boy feeling? Is that a happy face? How does the little boy or girl feel?" It can help you recognize your own feelings as a parent, too.

When I was 34 years old, I felt like a failure as a parent because of my rage. So I took a course of parenting. It was 6 weeks long, one night a week. I recommend a course in parenting to every parent, every grandparent and every teacher in this room to take these courses at least once in your life time. One night we spent 2 hours talking about feelings. It was like they were talking a strange language to me. I couldn't identify my feelings at all. I had written a story in 1973 about a little bird who learned to fly. It was a story of my life as a little girl. I didn't know what to do with it after I had written it so I hid it in my drawer. But after I went home from the parenting course, I took out that story and I read it again. 'Skylark' is the name of my story. Skylark is the bird who couldn't fly. When I read it again, I saw that Skylark did not express his feelings of being abused. So I had written 15 pages with no feeling words in it. I had described people, plot, events, and story, but my characters didn't use any feeling words. All I could do was an intellectual exercise. I wrote in the feelings that Skylark would be expected to feel. But I still could not feel my feelings. I didn't know it, but this was a major turning point in my life because I began to notice the times that I wasn't allowing my children to express their own feelings. This was in 1976.

To be able to share your feelings with another human being, you would have to be able to trust them. I did not trust others with my feelings because I had been abused when I tried to share them and, also, because my father sexually abused me when I was 2 through 8 years old. I kept this a secret from my first husband in 9 years of marriage, and I kept it a secret from the man who was to become my second husband. Secrets like that destroy trust.

Fortunately, six months after we were married, we attended a weekend "Marriage Encounter" program during which we were to write out our feelings 3 times a day for 20 minutes and then discuss them privately. I felt compelled to trust my husband and tell my secret. I had thought that no one would want me if they knew, but I overcame that fear and wrote him a letter, pouring out my heart and my secret to him. Then I waited while he read it.

What would his response be? Would he turn away from me? Would he not think me worthy to be his wife? None of that happened. He said, "Now I understand why you wrote your Skylark story and present it to groups and organizations. I didn't understand before but now it fits." I was 39 years old and I had finally told someone my secret. But my feelings were still blocked, locked up, and ice cold.

It took me until I was 46 yrs. old to express my feelings. Those extra feelings, all of the rage of feelings were connected to my telling the secret of sexual abuse when I was a child. Until I told my secret in a support group hundreds of times and had the injustice validated hundreds of times, all those feelings were blocked. And I had to grow up from a little girl who couldn't express feelings or identify them to an adult who could. I had to re-parent myself in this way by developing a feeling language.

One of the goals of parenting is to teach children to identify and name their feelings. 15 yrs. old is about the age of maturity. By 15, 16, 17 yrs. old, a child should be able to express their feelings and identify them. But that's not the final goal. The final goal is that when the child becomes an adult, all those feelings must be governed and regulated by love, compassion, and virtues. Love, compassion, and virtues should be an umbrella over all those feelings. Because feelings are like energy in our body. They cause us to have a biological, psychological experience. That energy has to be expressed in appropriate ways. Running, jumping, sports, talking, sometimes I have to hit a pillow. When I would get angry at work, I would go into the bathroom, and run in place. One day I raged at my boss. After 8 yrs. of working for him, I raged at him. Then I yelled

"I'M GOING HOME, NOW." And he said, "Are you coming back tomorrow?" I said, "YES!" Then I went home and couldn't eat. I couldn't sleep. I worried all night long because I had to go back to work the next morning. The very next morning, I was entering the radio station I worked at like a scared puppy, and he was waiting right there for me. I walked up to him and said, "I am sorry I got mad at you yesterday." He said, "You have nothing to apologize, for you were just expressing your feelings." He understood.

And the next week, a man came to be interviewed on a live program about a book he had written, called "All the rage". He was going to give a seminar that weekend on anger. I decided to take his seminar. I studied anger from different sources for 7 yrs. And I began to teach Anger Alternatives at the college. I stopped raging at my children.

How young can you tell to teach children about feelings? At what age? I can give you an example, a story about my sister. She and her 3 yrs. old daughter were visiting us for Christmas. All the adults were gathered together in the living room talking. And my niece, Natalie came running into the room screaming. My sister put her arms around Natalie. She said, "Tell mama, I'm frightened of the helicopter." My sister was teaching my 3 year old toddler niece about feeling language. And my little niece said, "I'm frightened, Mommy." And another time, I saw my sister looked at my 3 yrs. old niece and said, "You look sad, are you?" And this little girl could affirm that. My sister then had the opportunity to ask my niece, "What are you sad about? What has happened?"

This is teaching children to identify feelings. There is a story of Belinda. I was sitting at a table at a conference in N.Y. A woman was telling a story of her daughter who was 6 years old. Her daughter's name was Belinda. The mother was away at an evening event and a babysitter was taking care of Belinda. When she came home, the babysitter was left, he was a man. But it could just as well have been a woman. And Belinda said, "I hope Derrick doesn't ever touch me where he did again." And the mother's heart began to beat very fast. "Where did he touch you?" She said, "Right here," pointing to her pubic area. "How do you feel?" she said. She keyed in the feeling words immediately. Belinda at 6 years old could tell her mother, "I feel Yucky." "Do you want to talk about it?" "No, I just want to go to bed", she said. "Well, we'll put you to bed, but if you want to talk about it in the future, I have a special friend who would love to talk about this with you."

The point is Belinda was allowed and invited to express her feelings. She had been taught to express her feelings. I don't know how 'yucky' translates into Japanese, but it can translate into 'disgusting'. Now Belinda is a grown up woman about 19, 20 years old and she is healthy, because she was allowed and encouraged to express her feelings at 6 years old and the situation was not buried. These are just 2 examples of teaching children to identify and express their feelings. Those who are aware of feelings and have not buried the shame of abuse or fear of bullying can heal faster.

A great educator named Abdu'l-Baha was once asked, "What is the purpose of life?" He said, "The purpose of life is to develop the virtues." My message today is not only to encourage children to share their feelings, but to encourage them to learn the virtues at the same time. One virtue that I have had to learn is 'forgiveness'. At some point in my journey of healing, I learned to forgive my mother and father. Remember earlier I said that the goal of childhood is to identify all the feelings. Then the goal after 15, 16, 17 years old is to have love, compassion, and virtues to be an umbrella over all those feelings. Because feelings are just feelings, they just tell us about what is going on inside of us. They do not determine our behavior. And choices must be made based on virtues as we regulate our feelings. We have much to learn from who had been abused. People who had been abused have difficulties with the virtue of 'trust'. They have difficulties with 'forgiveness'. But they can teach us much about the virtue called 'detachment'. Detachment can lead us to purity of motive. Detachment can lead us to peace. Detachment can lead us to understanding of our behavior and choosing behavior, and can lead to world peace. I believe that the suffering people of the world can teach us much about peace, too. If you look at the list of feelings, you'll see some of them seem to be negative. Some of them might be feelings that bullies have. The reason they are there, is so that we will learn that human beings have two natures. We have a spiritual nature or higher nature. And we have lower nature. The feeling that you read on the handout that might be negative, might be expressed by our lower nature. That is why we need the virtues. If we are compassionate, we may not be indignant when someone injures our feelings. If we look into ourselves, we would know that we have the same feelings that any other human being has. Our great educator and philosopher said, "All the people of the world are one." Many educators have said to be kind to your enemy. So I'm going to end this program this afternoon with thanking you for coming. I think I've run out of things to say. So if you have any question, I'll take questions now. I'll think immediately of things to say. Thank you.

Question: When my child showed his/her anger, I said to him/her why he/she is so mad at such a simple thing. Eventually he/she ended up with that he/she doesn't want to talk about it anymore. I think there might be a boundary of a child as a human being, and no one is not allowed to invade it without his/her permission. How do you think about it?

Answer: If a child shows his/her anger, please ask him/her, "Are you mad? You seem to be mad, are you?" And say, "Sometimes mom gets mad, too.

Let's show angry faces together." I've created some children songs. I'll sing one of them for you.

"Let your inside feeling match your outside face. So you don't become invisible. Learn to share your feelings when you really get mad, and you won't feel so terrible. It's a sad, sad feeling to be all alone. When you need a hug, but your heart's a stone. So tell a friend what's deep inside. It's Ok if you want to cry. (Name) you can't hide, so let your feeling show outside."

Let them know that it's not the anger that is bad. It's the behavior. I know 18 yrs. old boy was so angry that he put his fist through the wall and made a hole in it. The anger wasn't wrong. But he needs it to have an opportunity to express without his mother getting mad at him and without destroying things. He needs to express it in appropriate ways. Don't be afraid of anger. Face the fire. Face the dragon. So you can encourage them to regulate their feelings.

Question: I sometimes feel guilty or incapable as a parent…

Answer: You need to develop forgiveness for yourself as a parent. We are taught in many cultures to blame ourselves for whatever goes wrong. Women are the first educators of children. So therefore, they feel that they are doing everything wrong. They don't usually have enough support. But you are doing a good job. We blame ourselves and we allow others to blame us. Would you forgive your best friend? Would you forgive your child? If you can, then you can forgive yourself. Parents need support. That is why you are bound together as parents and teachers. The answer isn't blame. The answer is tools and powers. I blamed myself for 15 yrs. and finally I went to a parenting course. My mind exploded with new ideas. Then I went home to try to use it. My 12 year old son said, "Oh, mommy, you just learned that out of a book." And I did. There is a woman's poster that I created. I want to tell you about.

"If a woman pursues her good against all odds, Under the harsh gaze of all those she loves, All those who love her, all those who don't care for her, Even those who don't know her... Giving them their right to judge her every moment, Every memory, every mistake on the way... And still find a way to love herself, Take responsibility for her growth, And continue pursuing her good, and the greater good, She will find that her self-esteem is a light that radiates from within, not from without! I have this and I wish it for you."[xxxiv] When I wrote that, memorized it, and reflected on it daily, I had the courage to stand up to the judgments of anybody. I stand up with the judgment of my parents. I stand up with the judgment of my brothers and sisters. If I didn't, I wouldn't be gone from my husband for 2 weeks. I'm a tough lady! (laughter)

Question: Recently I am trying to conquer or overcome anger. I used to show my feeling only by my behavior, but I realized that it makes much easier if I use words openly express my feelings. For example: When I was tired, I never expressed it to my children but acted irritated when I was tired. Now I tell them that I am tired and without telling any further my children began to help me. Don't you think it has related to your talk?

Answer: Yes, it does have a strong relationship to what I said. Mothers and Fathers can't put themselves upon pedestals. My mother never said, "I'm tired." Consequently, I worked till I hurt my body. I didn't know I was tired. It is healthy to tell children what you are feeling. It's not healthy, however, to lean on children emotionally. It's not healthy for the Mama to tell children, "I'm depressed." We have friends for that. Relatives, husbands, sisters and brothers can help, too. Children are too young and tender hearted to deal with such problems. They don't have the emotional resources to deal with such problems. They are naturally empathetic. Emotions are not to be repressed. They are not to be controlled. They are simply to be regulated. Do you see the difference between that? We always have different feeling impulses. They give us information about ourselves.

If a 10 year old boy, like the woman said, is expected to control his/her anger 24 hrs. a day, he would eventually explode. When I exploded at my boss, I was fortunate that he understood feelings. If a 10 year old boy exploded in the school compound, it's a different story. So children need outlets for anger.

Question: What do you think about the social factors that cause more of those abuse cases to happen?

Answer: The world is gaining greater awareness. These things have been going on for centuries and decades in secret. In the USA, one out of 4 girls is sexually abused. One out of 7 boys are molested before they are 16 or 18. In South Africa, in the report of the cases of child sexual abuse, 33% of it is done by the school teachers. In India, 25% of the population has been sexually abused before the age of 16. There is child sexual slavery in India and Thailand. (There are similar reports on other countries, too.) In Brazil, a child is sexually abused in every 30 minutes.[34] It is a world wide epidemic. The reason that I give you the statistics is to tell you that though I'm not a healer, I teach people prevention. I have another program that teaches prevention. Sharing feelings is an integral part of prevention. So it addresses the social problems. We can't be a world society or world global society of people who do not express their feelings. What you see around the world right now is but rage and war. Look at the

---

[34] These statistics are taken off the internet at Google. Just type in Sexual Abuse Statistics with the name of the country and you will be directed to the information.

youth who rioted in France in 2005, the Arab Spring, the rebelling in Turkey. Look at the fact, that there are 400,000 cases of bullying reported each year in a so called civilized country like Great Britain. These are angry children. So I implore you as parents and teachers to teach your children to express their feelings openly.

Question: Do you think have there been these cases before and just recently does it reveal its reality owe to the IT development?

Answer: It has been there before. The world is going through a moral crisis right now. Each school, each family and each community has to address the moral issues of the days in which we live. We can't live in a moral free society. And we can't be morally neutral. That is why I travel and teach. I could stay home and just watch TV. I taught in China last year where I spoke at the UNESCO conference and presented a program called Protective Behaviors for Children. And I stayed 5 extra days, so I could teach teachers and principals the Protective Behaviors in the class room setting. I hear Japan has a wonderful program that they have implemented called CAP (Child Abuse Prevention). Australia is the leader in child abuse prevention. We have to realize that sexual abuse of children was not common knowledge until a ground breaking book came out in 1979: *"Conspiracy of Silence."* That's when the media grabbed hold of it and talk shows started sensationalizing it *and the field of psychology began to grow*

*in that direction. Survivors of Incest Annonymous, a 12 step
program was developed world wide.* Victims and survivors
had nothing before 1979

Question: I am teaching the 6th grade, 41 children.
The list of virtues is very useful. But I am struggling
teaching children morals because they can't catch the
meaning of virtues. They are just joking around and
can't take it seriously. It seems chaos to me. Do you
have any suggestion for this?

Answer: There is a wonderful book called "Family
virtues guide". Please refer to:
http://www.virtuesproject.com for more
information. Treating virtues as a joke happens in
America, too. This virtues project has exercises,
games, and projects. It can guide the teachers in
teaching virtues in many ways. Parents, teachers,
and communities, all have to work together. Parents
are taught to be educated in virtues and demonstrate
them at home. The teacher has to be educated in
virtues and demonstrate patience, forgiveness and
firmness. The small community needs to be
informed, so that parents work together and teachers
work together with the children. As far as children
losing their interest, I know that children today have
very short attention spans. And the media affects the
children's attention span. I'm not blaming the media,
but everything like feelings has to be regulated and
to be moderated. If a child watches TV 4, 5 hrs. a
day, they don't get a chance to express their feelings.
They are like Zombies. Parents watch TV 4 hrs. a

day, they are like Zombies, too. They miss opportunities to have family intimacy. And it's so hard when there are so many children.

Question: We have children from Elementary and Junior High schools in our community. There are some children who have troubles within their hearts. They tend to exclude other children and tell lies. But I don't want to label the children as bad children. I prefer to treat them as equal. How should I treat these children? Do you know any best ways?

Answer: Tough question. I repeat. The world is going through the moral crisis right now. Our job is to show kindness to everyone. And show compassion and love to everyone. Are you worried about protecting your own children? (No...) I pray for people that I am worried about. And I teach whatever corner of the world I find myself in. I'm here to teach you about feelings, prevention of bullies. I wish I could heal bullies. There are a lot of bullies in the world I would like to heal. The world is going through a moral crisis. And my part is the prevention and teaching about feelings and virtues. And virtues can help. Virtues must be taught simultaneously with feelings because of our dual nature...a physical nature and a spiritual nature. Reach the children you can and trust in a higher reality. Thank you.

The Importance of Feelings Workshop Outline

I.   Opening: The Importance of a Feeling Language

II.   Do the Feeling Word Test

III. Hand out the Sheet with Faces that represent Feelings. Have them fill it out in Japanese.

III. Hand out the Sheet of Feeling Words (www.skylarkpubl.com)

IV.   Story of Natalie

V.   Story of Belinda

VI.   Introduction to Alice Miller's Work: "Thou Shall not be Aware".

VII. Feelings and their connection to Boundaries: Go through the first sequence of the Boundary Sculpting Game. Ask for memories of Feelings.

VIII. Closure and Questions

Free handouts for this program can be found at my website:
www.skylarkpubl.com   Look under Free Materials.

Note: Excerpts from "Assisting the Traumatized Soul" and "Healing the Wounded Soul" used by permission of the National Spiritual Assembly of the Baha'is of the United States of America.

Chapter Six will illustrate how one mother encouraged her adopted son to express his feelings openly rather than hit his younger brother in anger because he was afraid his real mother wouldn't be able to find him if they moved to another neighborhood. Upon first glance at "Randy and Butch Learn to Discharge Anger," one would be tempted to call this "bullying behavior," but examination at a deeper level reveals the torment under the surface that Randy is hiding.

Chapter Six

Randy and Butch Learn to Discharge Anger, (Anger Alternatives)

For Junior Youth

KwaZulu-Natal, South Africa

Slam!

Randy hit his brother hard and shoved him inside the door to the kitchen.

"Leave me alone!" said Bradley as he stumbled over Rocky, their dog.

"Boys, wash your hands. It's time for supper," Mom said as she wiped her hands on her apron. "And stop hitting your brother, Randy!"

"I'm not hungry!" Randy took the steps two at a time and bolted through the hallway to his bedroom. He plopped down on the bed and looked around.

Everything was so familiar and comfortable. This was his room. His house. His neighborhood—and now, he had to move.

"They can't make me! This house is good enough," he scowled.

He had a funny feeling inside but he couldn't name it. He always had this feeling. He had it when he thought about his real mother. It was so hard to remember her, especially since he didn't see her very often.

He also had this "feeling" when someone yelled at him and when the dog next door barked. He could make the feeling go away by playing basketball in the back yard, by going to the movies, and sometimes with an ice cream cone. But it always came back when things were real quiet, or when he had problems, like right now.

"I don't like it when it's quiet," he thought.

Randy turned on his radio. Why did they have to move?

Randy's mother came up the stairs and knocked on his door.

"Who is it?" he asked.

"It's Mom. May I come in?"

"Sure, go ahead."

"It's time to eat, Randy," Mom said gently.

"I told you! I'm not hungry!"

"It's the move, isn't it?"

"I don't want to move, Mom! I like this house."

"Bring it up at the family meeting after supper."

"Family meetings are stupid!"

"Please come downstairs and eat," she urged.

"Oh, all right," he said sullenly.

The neighbor's dog started barking. He barked all through supper. Randy hated to hear the dog bark like that.

He looked out the window. The dog was tied up as usual. A ten-foot chain pulled tight against the dog's neck. He had worn the grass all around him in a ten-foot area. That was his world. Too small, too tight, too suffocating.

Randy had that feeling again, this time in his throat and chest. Why would anyone do that to an animal? Twenty-four hours a day. Tied up with no walks, barely enough food to eat.

The dog was thin, uncared-for. Randy thought about turning the old woman in to the humane society.

His mother was talking now and her voice broke into his thoughts. "Dad will be gone on business for about one more week. It'll be nice to have him back home." Mom looked at Randy. "What are you thinking about, Randy?" she asked.

"The dog. It bothers me when he barks like that."

"I know. I hate to see anything tied up like that myself. It makes me feel sick to my stomach. How do you feel, Randy?"

"I feel confused. I get a funny feeling inside. Like I want to ... to ... " He broke off and blinked his eyes.

"Like you want to what?" she said.

"Oh, who cares?"

"I care," she said gently.

"No, you don't. You're not my real mother."

"I really care about you and the dog, Randy! Maybe if we all talked together, we could figure out something to do about the dog. Why don't you bring it up at the family meeting? But until then, you could bring some of Rocky's food over to the dog."

Randy jumped up and ran out the kitchen door to the back porch. He filled up an old plastic container and started walking across the back yard to Mrs. Master's yard.

The dog rose to his feet as Randy approached. Off in the distance, Randy heard a siren blaring faintly. He moved toward the dog.

The dog growled, untrusting.

"I'm not going to hurt you!"

The dog snapped and lunged at him.

The sound of the siren grew louder, stronger.

Randy inched closer to the dog trying to calm him. "Easy boy, easy. I'm just trying to feed you."

The siren was deafening now.

The dog turned its head and sniffed the air to see what the siren meant. Randy quickly shoved the food just inside the dirt circle and ran to the side of the house.

Paramedics were setting up a stretcher and rolling it to the neighbor's front door.

Randy stood off to the side watching the man and woman work.

When they knocked at the door, Mrs. Master's daughter opened it and asked them to come in. They carried in the stretcher while other neighbors joined Randy outside.

"What's wrong?" they asked him.

"I don't know. I came out to feed the dog because he seemed hungry, and all of a sudden, the paramedics showed up," he said.

After a few minutes, the paramedics carried the old woman out of the house and placed her in the ambulance.

Great, thought Randy as he watched the ambulance pull away with the siren sounding. *Now what's gonna happen to the dog?*

Mrs. Master's daughter came out of the house and saw Randy looking at Butch. "Excuse me, young man. Would it be possible for you to take care of Butch while my mother is in the hospital? He's a good dog and he's never hurt anyone. Though he does make a lot of noise. I have a cat at home that doesn't like dogs. And Butch is so big, he'd be cooped up in my small apartment anyway," she said.

"I'm sure we can take care of him, Ma'am. I'll ask my mom right away." Randy ran back to his house and yelled, "Mom, let's get this family meeting started. There's an emergency. The ambulance just took old Mrs. Master to the hospital and I want to talk about her dog, Butch."

Mom smiled. After two months of her hoping and encouraging that he would, Randy was finally going to join them. Why, she wondered, did it always take a crisis to move people to act?

"Ok," mom said. "Bradley, you were the chairman last time, so I'll be the chairperson this time since this is Randy's first meeting. And the first thing we'll do is pass around a few compliments. Bradley, that was very thoughtful of you to wash the dishes yesterday when Randy had to do his homework. Randy, I like it when you take such an interest in animals. You've always taken good care of Rocky!"

"Thanks for fixing Jello tonight, Mom. It's my favorite!" said Bradley.

"You're welcome, Bradley."

They both looked at Randy.

Bradley smiled, "Thanks for letting me borrow your ball glove, Randy. That was nice of you to share it with me!"

"Yeah, sure," Randy felt embarrassed. This was awkward for him. "Now I'm supposed to say something nice to Bradley and you?"

"That's right. Can you think of anything?" Mom asked.

"Well, thanks for doing the dishes for me last night while I did my homework."

He couldn't think of anything to say to Mom so he grew silent.

The dog next door started barking again. He was straining at his chain and his bark sounded husky.

Mom read the notes from the last meeting. "Anybody have anything to add to this?"

Nobody said anything.

"Any old business?" she asked.

"I'm confused," said Randy.

"First we have compliments, then we read the notes from last week and discuss old business. If there isn't any, we go on to new business. It looks like we've got several things on the agenda for new business."

"Yeah, like our move and the dog!" said Randy.

"What would you like to discuss first, Randy?" Mom encouraged.

"The dog! Butch is tied up with no one to feed him or care for him. The old woman's been taken to the hospital. Mrs. Master's daughter says she can't take care of Butch because her apartment is too small and she has a cat. She said Butch has never hurt anyone. When I went out to feed him, I noticed that his collar is too tight. He's got sores all over his neck with lots of flies bothering him."

"That's terrible!" said Bradley. "What can we do, Mom?"

"What do you think should be done, Randy?" asked mom.

"I think we should take him to the vet, first. Get some medicine for his neck," said Randy.

"Mom, I could buy Butch a new and bigger collar," said Bradley.

"Can we get close enough to him to put on a new collar and take him to the vet?" asked Mom.

"I don't know. He snapped at me when I tried to feed him. Maybe he was just hungry. Maybe he needs to go for a walk after being tied up for so many years. All the kids in the neighborhood are afraid of him because he barks and growls and howls so much," said Randy.

"Yes, he seems like a very angry dog," said Mom.

Just then the dog let out a pitiful howl.

"He's in pain, Mom—not just angry!" said Randy.

She looked at her perceptive son. The dog's not the only one in pain, she thought.

"Ok, is it agreed that we go to the pet store tonight to buy a new collar and tomorrow morning, Saturday, we bring the dog to the veterinarian?" Mom asked.

Both boys nodded.

"Next new business," she said. "I guess that would be our upcoming move."

"I don't want to move, Mom," said Randy.

"Randy, you're at the age when I've started letting you make some important decisions. Do you remember the way your father and I set that up?"

"Yes, you said as long as I don't hurt anyone, damage any property, or place myself in danger, there are some choices I can make for myself," Randy said as he lowered his eyes.

"That's right! We want you to learn how to make some decisions now while you're young so that when you grow up, you'll know how to make good decisions. That's one reason we have family meetings. So you can see how adults discuss things before they make a decision. And we also said that there are some decisions that your father and I will have to make for both of you boys. Such as the move into our new home that will be closer to where your father works—a home that will have more room for you to grow in. We <u>are</u> going to move, but there are many decisions that will have to be made regarding that move. We will need your help in making those decisions, and in planning the move."

Randy felt that feeling in his throat and chest again. "But I ... I ... " Randy stopped.

His mother looked at him gently and encouraged him to continue. "What is it, Randy? What are you feeling? Use an 'I-feel' sentence."

"I ... I feel confused because I'm feeling so many things and I can't sort them out," he said.

"Pick out one then, and start with that," she said.

"Ok, I know I feel worried! I'm worried that my real mom might not be able to find me if we move. I'm worried about the dog, too."

"All right. We'll tell everyone who knows your real mother to give her our new address when they hear from her. And every time you feel worried, I want you to come to me and tell me about it so we can talk with each other just like we are right now," Mom said.

"Did you know that when we have strong feelings like worry, fear and anger that it causes us to be charged up with energy? We get charged up with energy when hurtful things happen to us, too, or when we feel frustrated. We need to get rid of that extra energy or it will hurt our bodies. Sometimes we even turn on others with it and hurt them. There are many ways to get that energy out—by talking about the problem, crying, writing, or shaking. Some people even hit a pillow," said Mom.

"Mom! That's what's wrong with Butch! He's been chained up for a long, long time now and he barks and snarls at everyone! He's got a lot of anger energy!" exclaimed Randy.

"You could be right about that, Randy. When we don't get rid of that anger energy, we sometimes hurt others with it. Getting rid of the energy is called discharging. But discharging doesn't work if you do something bad or mean to other people. You have to discharge it in a safe way, like crying or talking about what made you feel hurt," she said.

"Mom, I'm gonna help Butch discharge his anger energy!" said Randy.

"Good! I hope you can. But be careful. I wouldn't want Butch to bite you! Now I think we've covered all the new business. So I'll hand out your allowance and serve a treat. How do brownies and ice cream sound?" she asked.

"So this is what a family meeting is like. Not bad, Mom!" Randy grinned.

After they finished eating their dessert, Mom and Bradley went to the pet store to buy a new collar. Randy went up stairs, took a shower and got ready for bed. He could hear the dog howling outside. It made him feel sad. The dog sounded lonely and sad, too.

The next morning, Randy got up early, ate breakfast, and went out to the back yard.

Butch started barking at him.

Randy moved closer, talking to him. "Easy boy. I'm your friend. I'm not going to hurt you. You've just been tied up alone for too long.

The dog lunged at him.

Randy moved back, picked up a stick, and reached out toward the dog with it. The dog grabbed it and growled while he shook the stick violently back and forth. His head was a blur, it moved so fast!

"That's it, Butch! Now you're discharging. Mom says you've got to get rid of this energy, but you can't hurt anyone else with it."

Randy grabbed the stick and threw it into the center of the dirt circle. The dog ran after it, picked it up with his teeth, and shook it violently again.

"Good job! Now you're getting the hang of it," said Randy.

Randy ran back to his yard and got another container of dog food from the back porch. He brought it up to the dog.

The dog was still shaking the stick. Now it came over to Randy and sniffed the food. This time, he let Randy approach without trying to attack him.

Randy put the food down and backed up while the dog ate.

"The old woman didn't even get a chance to say good-bye to you, did she?" he said wistfully. "My real mother didn't say good-bye to me, either. Nobody asked me what I wanted. Nobody explained what was going on."

Randy felt like crying. A tear rolled down his cheek. He dried it right away on the back of his shirt sleeve.

Bradley came up to Randy. He was carrying the new collar and a leash.

Randy punched him in the arm.

"OWw!" cried Bradley. "That hurt!" Tears came to Bradley's eyes.

Randy looked at the hurt look in Bradley's eyes. Then he thought about Butch. Randy realized that he was helping the dog discharge his feelings so he won't hurt anyone. But he had also just hurt Bradley so that he could stop himself from crying.

Mom said crying was one way of discharging hurt feelings.

Is that why I'm always hitting Bradley? he wondered thoughtfully. I was thinking about my real mother and feeling sad and confused inside. And instead of talking or crying about how I felt, I hit him.

"Bradley, I'm sorry I hit you. Would you help me put the new collar on the old woman's dog?" he asked.

Bradley took a step backward, "I will if you don't hit me again!"

"I'm not going to hit you. Here, you hold the stick out to the dog and I'll work on taking the old collar off," said Randy.

The dog growled real low.

"Easy boy! Take the stick. We're not going to hurt you."

Butch took the stick and shook it hard.

Randy quickly grabbed the collar and unbuckled it.

Butch yelped. Suddenly free of any restraint, the dog took off as fast as lightning with Randy and Bradley chasing as fast as they could.

Randy thought, He's not just running. He's discharging anger energy after all those years of being tied up.

The dog ran toward the quarry near their home, barking all the way.

"Bradley, hook the leash to the new collar and as soon as we get to the quarry, you head for the big rock and I'll go toward the tree. Maybe we can trap him in the middle near the cliff!"

"Ok, Randy!" said Bradley, running hard and out of breath.

Randy picked up a good-sized throwing stick on the way to the tree. When Bradley reached the rock, Randy threw the stick to the dog.

Butch lunged at it and both boys ran to him. Randy held the dog while Bradley buckled the collar around his neck. Then they walked him back toward home.

Mom was out on the front porch looking in all directions for them.

"There you are! I've been looking for you. It's time to take the dog to the clinic. Can you get him into the car?" she asked.

Bradley got in the car first and pulled on the leash while Randy pushed at the other end. Everything was fine except that Butch sat on Bradley during the whole trip to the vet.

The dog started to howl over and over again.

Bradley covered his ears.

Mom looked in the back seat.

"It's ok, Mom," Randy said. "He's just discharging."

Mom laughed, 'Well, I've got some feelings I'd like to share with that dog, too!"

Once inside the clinic, the dog was fine.

Dr. Javadid was surprised to see the strange dog as he was expecting Rocky. But he treated the dog's neck and gave them some antibiotics for him.

"Why this is Mrs. Master's dog, Butch, isn't it?"

Butch turned his head at the mention of his name.

"Yes, she's our neighbor," said Bradley.

"I had heard she was in the hospital and was expected to go into the nursing home temporarily. I was wondering who was taking care of her dog," said Dr. Javadid.

Bradley and Randy looked at each other. "That means Butch is going to need a new home for a while," said Randy.

"It looks like it," said Mom. "But we'll talk more about that on the way home. Good-bye, Dr. Javidid. Thanks for your help."

Bradley, Randy, Butch, and Mom walked back to the car.

"Well, Randy, we have another decision that has to be made. How will we take care of Butch? We've already got one dog," she said as they all got into the car.

"Mom, I feel sick and confused whenever Butch is tied up. I just don't have the heart to tie him up again. He needs freedom. He needs to be able to act like a real dog. Since we can't keep him at our house, could we bring him out to Uncle Jake's farm? He could run loose and have plenty of freedom there."

"That's a wonderful idea!" said Mom. "Let's take a drive out to Uncle Jake's right now and see what he says," she said as she headed down the highway towards the farm.

Randy thought a lot about Butch during the ride to Uncle Jake's. He thought about Butch being tied up for years. He thought about Butch's anger. He thought about his own anger and about how often he hit his brother.

If Butch can discharge his anger, so can I, Randy decided. It's not fair if I hurt Bradley instead of discharging my anger, frustration, fear."

He had a sudden flash of a memory of a small defenseless boy being tied up and he felt sad. He started crying. "Mom, could you stop the car? I think I need to discharge some sadness," said Randy.

Mom looked to see if it was safe, then pulled over and stopped the car. Then she got in the back seat with Randy, Bradley, and Butch.

She held Randy in her arms while he cried. Butch whimpered and licked Randy's tears.

"Mom, I've been hitting Bradley instead of discharging my hurt feelings. I've been so angry and frustrated lately. I'll try not to hit him anymore, but could you help me with my anger?"

189

"I sure will. Your dad will help, too. You know, sometimes your dad and I will get angry with you and Bradley. But before we talk with you and try to deal with the problem, we discharge most of our anger so we don't hit you or hurt you with our words."

"How do you do that?" he asked.

"By talking it out with each other or writing a letter to each other. Sometimes I get so frustrated that I cry, too. And I've hit my share of pillows when I feel angry."

"I'm glad it's ok to cry, Mom," said Randy.

"You bet it is! Feeling better?" she asked.

"Yes. Let's go to Uncle Jake's!"

"Ok. His farm is just up the hill and around the curve."

"I sure hope Uncle Jake will take Butch," said Randy.

"Me, too," said Bradley.

"All we can do is ask," Mom said. "There he is now up at the mail box." Mom honked the horn and Uncle Jake looked up as they pulled up to the drive leading to the farmhouse.

"Hi, Uncle Jake!" yelled Randy and Bradley.

"Hi, yourself! What brings all of you out to the farm?" asked Uncle Jake. And who's that in the back seat with you boys? That's not Rocky!"

Mom spoke first. "Well, our neighbor, Mrs. Master, was taken to the hospital unexpectedly. When she gets out, she'll have to go into a nursing home for a while. This is her dog, Butch. She was having a hard time caring for him. Her dog was tied up all the time. We were wondering if you'd mind keeping him here on the farm for a while? He's a good dog. Just needs a little attention, and a lot of room to run."

"I'd be glad to keep him out here, Sandy. What's his name again?" asked Uncle Jake.

"Butch!" said Randy.

Butch nuzzled Randy's arm and licked his face.

"Sure, old Butch can stay here with me. And if Mrs. Master has to stay in the nursing home permanently, I'll just adopt him."

"You hear that, Butch? You might be adopted, just like me! But Uncle Jake, you've got to promise me that you'll never tie him up and leave him," said Randy.

"That's a promise, Randy!" said Uncle Jake.

Randy looked at Mom and they both smiled their biggest smiles.

Bahá'í Consultation

"Bahá'í consultation can be defined as a process for producing a change in order to accomplish some definite purpose. This involves a sharing and interaction of thoughts and feelings in a spirit of love and harmony."[35]

---

[35] John E. Kolstoe, Consultation, George Ronald Publisher, © 1985, page 9

The story of Randy and Butch demonstrates Randy's sharing of his thoughts and feelings as he interacted with his mother and his brother to accomplish the purpose of helping the dog. While going through this process, he found and finally expressed the feelings of which he was not conscious—his need to cry and talk about the possible loss of his real mother. The entire family achieved a victory together.

Consultation supersedes the need for punishment but only if the individuals involved sincerely want to change their behavior and adopt the use of the following requisites of consultation:

"The prime requisites for them that take counsel together are purity of motive, radiance of spirit, detachment from all else save God, attraction to His Divine Fragrances, humility and lowliness amongst His loved ones, patience and long-suffering in difficulties and servitude to His exalted Threshold. Should they be graciously aided to acquire these attributes, victory from the unseen Kingdom of Bahá shall be vouchsafed to them."[36]

"If, in fact, 'violence' toward a woman or children continues, stronger measures must be taken. "Discipline of some sort, whether physical, moral, or

---

[36] 'Abdu'l-Bahá, Selections from the Writings of 'Abdu'l-Bahá, p. 86

intellectual is indeed indispensable, and no training can be said to be complete and fruitful if it disregards this element. ... While the physical discipline of children is an acceptable part of their education and training, such actions are to be carried out 'gently and patiently' and with 'loving care', far removed from the anger and violence with which children are beaten and abused in some parts of the world. To treat children in such an abhorrent manner is a denial of their human rights, and a betrayal of the trust which the weak should have in the strong in a Bahá'í community."[37]

The story of Randy and Butch was a true story. Randy (not his real name) went on to become a member of the military, then went to college and became an accountant, married, and has his own family now. Randy's mother had to set boundaries for him so that he would not keep hurting his younger brother. She also demonstrated "consultation" in their family gathering. This story is included as a means to help mothers and fathers understand the importance of training their children to not bully or be violent.

1. What if Randy's younger brother had been a younger sister and he had been hitting her instead? What human rights would have been

---

[37] Universal House of Justice, Violence toward Women and Children, 24th January 1993

denied her? What if it was an older sister who was bullying a younger sibling, male or female? What human rights would have been denied them? How could this be resolved through consultation? What kind of discipline would be appropriate?

2. Violence against women and children are condemned in the Bahá'í Faith. Does that include "bullying"? Give some examples of bullying, both verbal and physical.

3. What finally changed Randy's heart?

4. What is the value of consultation in families and communities?

5. What are some of the principles of consultation?

Here are 10 Declarations for the Human Rights of Children:

1. All children have the right to what follows, no matter what their race, color, sex, language, religion, political or other opinion, or where they were born or who they were born to.

2. You have the special right to grow up and to develop physically and spiritually in a healthy and normal way, free and with dignity.

3. You have a right to a name and to be a member of a country.

4.   You have a right to special care and protection and to good food, housing and medical services.

5.   You have a right to special care if handicapped in any way.

6.   You have a right to love and understanding, preferably from parents and a family, but from the government where these cannot help.

7.   You have a right to go to school for free, to play, and to have an equal chance to develop yourself and to learn to be responsible and useful.

8.   You have the right always to be among the first to get help.

9.   You have the right to be protected against cruel acts or exploitation, e.g. you shall not be obliged to do work which hinders your development both physically and mentally.

You should not work before a minimum age and never when that would hinder your health and your moral and physical development.

10. You should be taught peace, understanding, tolerance, and friendship among all people.

'Abdu'l-Baha received this question: What is the attitude of your belief toward the family? In His answer He used the word "virtue", which we need to remember is interchangeable with the word "power." This quotation has a bearing on the "rights" of each member of the family.

"Answer: According to the teachings of Bahá'u'lláh the family, being a human unit, must be educated according to the rules of sanctity. All the virtues must be taught the family. The integrity of the family bond must be constantly considered, and the rights of the individual members must not be transgressed. The rights of the son, the father, the mother -- none of them must be transgressed, none of them must be arbitrary. Just as the son has certain obligations to his father, the father, likewise, has certain obligations to his son. The mother, the sister and other members of the household have their certain prerogatives. All these rights and prerogatives must be conserved, yet the unity of the family must be sustained. The injury of one shall be considered the injury of all; the comfort of each, the comfort of all; the honor of one, the honor of all."[38]

---

[38] 'Abdu'l-Baha, "Promulgation of Universal Peace, Baha'i Publishing Trust, Wilmette, IL © 1982, p. 168

There are thousands of books about disciplining children, both secular and religious. And techniques for raising children are manifold. But something amazing happens when parents use the word of God to teach their children right from wrong instead of using abusive punishment. Watch what happens when the boy in this next story creates mischief for his two older sisters. The parents respond with moral principles from the Bahá'í Revelation, which instills in their minds and hearts an ability to develop a conscience that discerns right from wrong rather than focus purely on punishment for a wrong-doing. Likewise, if a boy is beaten for harming his sister, he will associate that beating with his sister rather than having an opportunity for the awakening of his conscience, and may ultimately seek revenge.

Chapter Seven

Chloe, the Elephant, (Conscience Development)

A Story for Children

Thailand

"Good morning, children!" Mom called up the stairs. "Are you ready for breakfast?"

Mother was especially cheerful because she not only had breakfast ready, but had also prepared devotions to start their day. She was going to teach the children about love, and Father was going to teach them about peace. She thought it was a wonderful way to start the day.

Chantel, Alexis, and Kevin came running down the stairs into the kitchen.

"What's for breakfast, Mom?"

"I'm hungry!"

"Can I have pancakes?"

Everyone was talking at once, pulling chairs out, reaching for napkins. Chantel was 8 years old, Alexis was 6, and Kevin was 5. He always wanted pancakes.

"Scrambled eggs and toast!"

"Great," said Father, "but first, some short devotions!"

"Devotions??? But I thought it was time to *eat?*" said Chantel.

"I'm hungry!" said Alexis.

"And I wanted pancakes!" grumbled Kevin.

"You can have pancakes tomorrow. Today we're having scrambled eggs," said Mother.

"Today's devotions are taken from *The Hidden Words* of Bahá'u'lláh, and *Paris Talks* by 'Abdu'l-Bahá." Father looked at Mother and motioned for her to begin.

"Bahá'u'lláh says: 'O Friend! In the garden of thy heart plant naught but the rose of love. And from the nightingale of affection and desire, loosen not thy hold.'"[39]

Father looked lovingly at each of his three children. "What does this mean?"

"That we should have roses of love in our hearts," answered Alexis. "And when Mama shows affection to me, she holds onto me and hugs me really tight," said Chantel.

Mother smiled. "This is what we want you to practice today, showing love and affection to each other."

"And the second part of our devotion today is from *Paris Talks*, which are talks that 'Abdu'l-Bahá gave in Paris in the early 20ᵗʰ Century. He said, 'I charge you all, that each one of you concentrate all the thoughts of your heart on love and unity. When a thought of war comes, oppose it by a stronger

---

[39] Hidden Words, Persian, #3

thought of peace. A thought of hatred must be destroyed by a more powerful thought of love. … If you desire with all your heart friendship with every race on earth, your thought spiritual and positive will spread. It will become the desire of others, growing stronger and stronger, until it reaches the minds of all men.'[40] What do you think about that?"

"Is that why you don't buy us toy guns and let us play war, Daddy?" asked Kevin.

"That's right, son. I want you to think about love and peace, like 'Abdu'l-Bahá says," Father said.

"Well, what if someone does something bad to us?" Alexis wondered. "Then you just tell your mother and father and we'll do our best to correct it," said Mother. "And now it's time to eat."

The children ate hungrily, but with good manners, saying "please pass the butter and jelly" and "please pass the salt and pepper".

After breakfast, Kevin went upstairs to play and the girls went outside to have a tea party in the rose garden with their giant bears, Fluffy Ears and Fuzzy Bones.

Their table was set with a tablecloth, plastic plates, saucers, and tea cups and there were 4 chairs, two for Chantel and Fuzzy Bones, and two for Alexis and Fluffy Ears.

Chantel was pouring tea when Kevin arrived in the garden with his stuffed animal, Bulldog.

---

[40] 'Abdu'l-Baha, Paris Talks, Baha'i Publishing Trust, London, © 1995, p. 29-30

"Can I join in the tea party?"

"No! There aren't enough chairs," said Alexis.

"We can sit on the grass," said Kevin.

"No! There's not enough room," Chantel said firmly.

Kevin felt sad. Then he felt mad! He felt left out. He ran to the house and up the stairs to his bedroom, kicked a ball that was in his way, and threw himself onto his bed.

And then, he started planning.

●

The girls played outside in the sunshine all day long, coming in for lunch for a short while and then returning to the rose garden. They played hopscotch. They built a tiny fort out of sticks and branches. Then they picked roses and asked Mother for a vase to put them in for their tea table. They played games all evening after supper; and then it was time for bed.

Kevin just smiled all day.

At 8 o'clock, Alexis came running into the kitchen and said, "Mama, I can't find Chloe, the Elephant, and I want to sleep with her tonight. Can you help me find her?"

"Have you looked in your closet, your toy box, and under your bed?" asked Mother.

"Yes, I have, but I can't find her anywhere!"

"Ok, let's everyone get together and look for Chloe," instructed Mother. So they looked!

They looked in the living room behind the sofa, under
the chair, in the dining room on top of each chair, in the kitchen cupboards, in the oven, in the refrigerator, in the basement where the washing machine and dryer were. They looked in the car, on the patio, behind the shower curtain, and under every bed. They looked everywhere! But they couldn't find Chloe.

Finally, Mother said, "Well, there's only one place I haven't looked." "Where?" asked Alexis who had tears in her eyes.
And Mother said, "The freezer!"
Mother slowly opened the door to the freezer—and there was Chloe,
now a solid block of ice!"

Alexis was crying now, "I want to sleep with Chloe!"

"Oh dear," said Mother. "You certainly can't sleep with Chloe tonight because she has to thaw in the kitchen sink overnight. Then we have to wring all the water out of her. Then we have to put her in the dryer and let her bounce around till she's all fluffy and dry again."

"I want to sleep with Chloe tonight!" wailed Alexis.

"Is there someone else you could sleep with?" Mother asked gently. "I ... I ... I could sleep with Fluffy Ears."

"Ok, you sleep with Fluffy Ears tonight."

"Now, let's go into the living room, so we can discuss what might have happened to Chloe," said Father.

They all went in and sat in a circle. Father spoke first. "Chantel, did you do this to Chloe?"

"No, Daddy, I would never do that to Chloe."

"Well," he said, "We know Alexis didn't do this to Chloe."

"I wanna sleep with Chloe!!!!" cried Alexis.

"We know that, Sweetheart, but remember, Fluffy Ears is very cuddly," said Mother.

"Kevin, did you do this to Chloe?"

"Yes, I did!" said Kevin, for he would never lie.

"Why did you do this to Chloe?" asked Father.

"Because Chantel and Alexis were having a tea party with Fluffy Ears and Fuzzy Bones and they wouldn't let me and Bulldog come."

And Mother asked, "How did you do this to Chloe?" for she was astonished at her 5-year-old.

"Well, when everyone was outside playing or working in the yard, I sneaked into Alexis' room and got Chloe and carried her to the kitchen and got a pan and carried her into the bathroom and filled up the pan with water and put Chloe in till she was soaky-squishy wet and put her in the pan and carried her to the kitchen and put her in the freezer and there she stayed all day long!" He said this all matter-of-factly, because he believed that his anger and his action were justified.

Mother and Father exchanged a tender look with one another.

"Poor Chloe," said Mother.

"Poor Chloe," said Chantel.

"Poor Chloe," said Father.

"What about me?" said Alexis. "I can't sleep with Chloe tonight!" she cried.

"I think you'll be able to sleep after we have devotions and consult about what happened today, don't you, Mother."

"That's a perfect idea!" said Mother, adding, "What did we learn this morning, during devotions?"

"We learned about love and peace from Bahá'u'lláh and 'Abdu'l-Bahá," said Chantel.

"And what did Bahá'u'lláh say in *The Hidden Words*, Chantel?"

"He said, 'In the garden of thy heart plant naught but the rose of love.'"

"Right," said Father.

"But we were in the rose garden showing love to each other," said Alexis.

"But did you show love to Kevin and include him in the tea party?" "No ...." The girls said together.

"And, Kevin, we talked about 'Abdu'l-Bahá in our devotions this morning. What did 'Abdu'l-Bahá say in *Paris Talks*?" Mother asked.

"He said something about our thoughts should be about peace."

"What kind of thoughts were you having, Kevin?" asked Father.

"My thoughts were being mean and mad," he said.

"What could you do with those kinds of thoughts?" asked Father. "Change them to thoughts of love?"

"Yes, and share them with your mother and father, too. Remember, 'Abdu'l-Bahá says, 'When a thought of war comes, oppose it with a stronger thought of peace' and 'if you desire with all your heart friendship, your thoughts will spread, growing stronger and stronger until they reach the minds of all men.' Bahá'u'lláh wants us to have unity in our family and to respect the human rights each person has of their property."

"Alexis, I'm sorry I put Chloe in the freezer," said Kevin.

"I feel sad that you did that to Chloe," said Alexis.

"And I felt angry when you wouldn't let me and Bulldog come to the tea party."

"And we're sorry we didn't let you join in the tea party with Fluffy Ears and Fuzzy Bones today," said Alexis.

"I know," said Chantel, "We can have another tea party tomorrow. Would you like that, Kevin?"

"Can Bulldog come, too?"

"Yes," the girls said together.

"And I'll bake cookies for the party," said Mother. "Now, let's say a prayer and off to bed with you."

"I'll say one," said Kevin. "O God! Guide me. Protect me. Make of me a shining lamp, and a brilliant star. Thou art the Mighty and Powerful."

"Thank you, Kevin, and thank you all for this wonderful consultation about love and peace and unity. Good-night now!"

All three children went up the stairs to bed. They washed their faces and brushed their teeth, and put on their pajamas, and tidied up their rooms.

Mother and Father read stories about 'Abdu'l-Bahá to them and tucked them in. Then they turned out the lights and they got ready for bed, too.

Two hours later, when the house was very still and everyone was asleep, one person was thinking about everything that happened that day.

She got out of bed and went down the hall way to Kevin's door. The nightlight was casting a faint ray of light across his trusting face. He was hugging Bulldog in his sleep.

Alexis was still angry. She thought about carefully lifting his arm and taking Bulldog to the freezer in the same way that Kevin had done to Chloe.

And then she thought about devotions that day and the stories about 'Abdu'l- Bahá, and how our thoughts of love and peace can become the desire of others, growing stronger and stronger, spreading all around the world.

She went back to her bed and she smiled as she laid her head on her pillow.

Questions for discussion:
1. Why were morning devotions important for Kevin, Alexis, and Chantel?
2. Did the parents in this story treat all three of their children equally even though two were girls and one was a boy?
3. Does God want ALL of his children to have devotions EVERY day?
   Why? What about adults?
4. What kept Alexis from doing the same things to Kevin while he slept?
5. Is problem-solving a family undertaking? In what way?
6. What are the principles of consultation that the Mother and Father used?
7. How did problem-solving with the word of God create peace in this family?
8. What prayer could Alexis say at the end of this story before she went to sleep?
9. How is problem-solving with consultation different than punishment?
10. How did the conscience of each child develop because the parents used the word of God?
11. What other powers did the children begin to recognize? When we talk to children about "right and wrong", can we call that the "Power of discernment"?

12. How can we talk to children about the "power of speech"? As the youngest one, what did Kevin need to learn about how to use his

power of speech, when things didn't go as he hoped or planned?

The End

****

In Chapter Eight, we will learn more about boundaries. Young people, girls and women need to be taught boundaries as they are growing up so that they will not experience boundary enmeshment which I have defined in this chapter. And so they can be true to their goals. We cannot "preach" chastity to youth unless we also give them knowledge of Boundaries. As adults we must show respect moment by moment for their boundaries.

Chapter Eight

The Boundary Sculpting Game

Make a copy of this section and cut the sections into separate pieces
For the group to play the Boundary Sculpting Game.

Boundary Enmeshment
(Violation)

It is defined as the uncomfortable and undesirable infringement and control of a person's identity, space, body, sexuality, possessions, emotions, thoughts, and their responsible freedom to express such. It is usually perpetrated by someone who does not recognize his or her own limits, treats others as objects rather than equals.

The ultimate remedy for boundary enmeshment or violation requires acknowledgement on the part of the violator; and re-establishment of autonomy, privacy, safety, comfort, reciprocity and unity.
Card 1

BOUNDARY VIOLATION CARD

I am the stranger, friend, co-worker, relative who hugs you without asking permission or checking to see if it is alright. This is an inappropriate hug that reflects the fact that I may be aroused because of watching or reading sexually explicit materials. There are over 400 chemicals in the brain, some of them there for the purpose of sexuality. I have not guarded myself or edited the content of materials that draw my attention, so I would not become stimulated by them. With this hug, I step inside your boundaries.

Card #2

BODY SENSATION CARD

A. I feel these sensations in my body: Chest muscles tighten, fist clenched, adrenalin racing, shallow breathing, hands shaking, headache, spastic colon, heart beating fast, asthma, face flushed or others. I do not recognize that this may be a boundary violation.

OR

B. I like it but my spiritual teachers have taught me that though this seems innocent, it is inappropriate if it arouses me sexually, teasing my biology. These sensations may lead me to question my teachings.

Card #3

THE MEDIA CARD THAT REPRESENTS THE CULTURE

Researchers for the Henry J. Kaiser Family Foundation in 1999 stated that when teens are most vulnerable to biological stimulation, they view approximately fourteen thousand sexual images and references on television, not including the rest of the media such as magazines, movies, music lyrics, the internet, and celebrity news stories PER YEAR! This can skew their perception of what life, people and sexuality are all about. The media teaches us that sexuality is uncontrollable. Sadly this information is almost ten years old and now we are seeing soft-porn in TV commercials.

Card #4

THE SPIRITUAL COMMUNITY
CARD

We are stronger in community. We can heal spiritually by experiencing God's mercy and grace within a community of believers that exemplify the teachings of God's Prophets, whether Hindu, Buddhist, Jewish, Christian, Muslim or Baha'i. Find out what true acceptance is in a community that seeks to nurture rather than judge. Gain knowledge daily from the Holy Word of God regarding what constitutes chastity and seek intimacy in a spiritual community.

Card #5

THE CHASTITY CARD

Modesty in all that pertains to dress, language, amusements, and all artistic and literary avocations. Purity, decency, clean-mindedness, and daily vigilance in the control of one's desires. Total abstinence from all alcoholic drinks, from opium, and from similar habit-forming drugs. It condemns infidelity in marital relationships, and all manner of promiscuity, of easy familiarity and sexual vices. It does not compromise with the standards, habits and excesses of a decadent age.
(Shoghi Effendi, ADJ, paraphrased)
Card #6

THE CHEERLEADER CARD

A2: Detach from your romantic feelings. Just because they were stimulated doesn't mean you have to fulfill them. They will fade away. They are not uncontrollable.

B2: Make a decision that is based on the Word of God.

C2: Be kind to yourself.

D2: Needs and wants are not faults.

E2: Acting in your own best interest is your hope for maintaining your chastity/purity.

F2: Taking a risk to share your feelings with members of your spiritual community will give you courage to be yourself and make discerning choices .

Card #8

THE CONFUSION CARD

A1. I have strong romantic feelings right now.

B1.   I'm going to hurt his/her feelings or he/she is going to get mad because of what I need or want.

C1. What will my friends think because I am different?

D1. I'm a terrible person because of these romantic feelings.

E1. I'm not ready for a sexual relationship. I'm in school and I want to go to college.

F1. Is it this hard for everyone to express what they are thinking and feeling about sex and chastity?

Card #7

THE AFFIRMATION CARD

I feel strong when I clearly define myself to you. You don't know who I am because I've been hiding my true belief system. I'm going to take a risk and tell you what I want so you will know what my boundaries are. You may feel uncomfortable feelings because of this challenge. I am growing in awareness and as I share my awareness with you, it will help you to grow, too. I believe in chastity before marriage and fidelity within marriage. I am objecting to the fact that you gave me a *hug* that was inappropriate. That type of hug is a challenge to my chastity.

Card #9

THE REALITY CARD

If I have been raised in an authoritarian family system, I may not have awareness of boundaries or rights. I may be a mixture of rigidity and permissiveness, and be caught up in the immorality of our culture. If so, I may be blind to your needs, feelings and boundaries. I feel awkward or threatened by your affirmation. I may try to intimidate you, force you, distract you, ignore you, shame you, rage at you, withdraw from you, or give you the silent treatment. Don't be fooled by any of this. Maintain your belief system, make discerning choices; and trust in God.

Card #10

THE FEELING CARD

These are many of the feelings I could have regarding this inappropriate hug and your negative response to my affirmation:

I feel angry, I feel anxious, I feel afraid, I don't feel safe, I feel worried, I feel trapped, I feel upset, I feel invaded, I feel uncomfortable, I feel unsure. I feel like power is being taken away from me. Sexuality is a power that I want to save for marriage. If you don't respect that, then I do not want you in my life.

Card #11

THE WHAT AM I LOOKING FOR CARD

I see the distress on your face. I hear the distress in your voice. You seem to be having strong feelings because of the inappropriate hug I gave you. It's OK to get angry with me. I will survive if you get angry. I will try to hear your anger with openness so we can work on our relationship. The more you tell me what your feelings are about the issue of chastity, the less I will violate your boundaries and the stronger we will become in maintaining our chastity. I recognize that we are stronger in a spiritual community and while doing service to the Cause of God.

Card # 12

THE TRUST CARD

With this act of trust in God and His commandments which are a mercy to me, I become more aware of the fact that I was depressed and confused, isolating myself and in denial of my participation in this inappropriate hug that caused me to have romantic feelings. I choose to share my feelings, needs and wants, repeatedly if necessary, with safe people, until I know that I am being heard. I have found my voice. I take responsibility for my behavior and I place chastity at the center of my heart. I practice Power in Purity because I want sex in marriage to be spiritual as well as physical!

Card #13

THE MEMORY CARD

Now I would like the group to sit down and discuss whatever memories came up for individuals. Talk about past experiences, current situations people are involved in and ideas the group has that work or don't work.

Card #14

Now that we have learned about boundaries, Chapter Nine will address "Protective Behaviors for Children." I believe that an aware child and an aware parent means a protected Child. The greater majority of adults who have been sexually abused, do not have awareness of how to set boundaries with others, therefore, their children are not protected. The workshop that follows has been presented in Japan, China, Thailand, Swaziland, Botswana, the Marshall Islands, KwaZulu-Natal in South Africa and in the United States.

Chapter Nine

Protective Behaviors for Children

I.   Introduction:

My name is Phyllis Peterson and I am a survivor of incest from the ages of 2 through 8 years old. The effects of this abuse have lasted for a life time because these were my developmental years in which sexuality and immorality was approved by a perpetrator that was the most important authority figure in my life, my father. I was a sexualized child which, I believe, led to my becoming bi-polar and acting out sexually as a teenager and adult.

This excerpt from my book "Assisting the Traumatized Soul: Healing the Wounded Talisman," shows you where I was 20 years ago: Please don't look too closely at me. You might see my secret. Please don't talk to me. I might accidentally tell you my secret. No, I don't want to be friends. Friends tell secrets. No, I don't want that promotion. I'm too occupied with my secret. And I can't express an opinion either. You might guess my secret. No, I'm not going to invite you to my home. We have a houseful of secrets! What's the sense of sharing feelings? People with secrets avoid them. And no, I can't tell you what my secret is. It's so secret, I may not be fully conscious of it.[41]

Being able to tell my secret hundreds of times within the safety of a support group helped to validate my experience and helped me to recognize that it was not my fault. Most survivors of incest believe, incorrectly that they were responsible for the abuse. Nothing could be farther from the truth.

My journey has led through a series of miss-diagnoses, wrong medication and a skewed perception of what life is truly meant to be....to a life that is fulfilling and creative, with relationships that are loving and trusting. In order for this to happen, I had to define and discover a just, nurturing authority and the importance of obedience to authority. I had to lead that sexualized child to grow and develop morally through a process of education. I wish that my education on sexual boundaries had begun when I was at least 3 years old. I am one of the fortunate ones. I

---

[41] Phyllis K. Peterson, "Assisting the Traumatized Soul: Healing the Wounded Talisman", Baha'i Publishing Trust, © 1999, page 5.

did receive an education and I attribute that education…and my growing faith and ever developing morality to the teachings of Baha'u'llah, who taught me to follow higher principles and to be obedient to the commandments of God.

Throughout my journey of healing I have attended many conferences on Child Abuse. I am here today to teach you what I have learned about how to protect children by making them aware of sexual boundaries. I am not a therapist but I can teach prevention. I can teach parents and children how to be aware of sexual boundaries. And I can train you in how to teach awareness of physical boundaries to children as young as 3 years old, children who are old enough to sit still and listen to a story and enjoy arts and crafts. There are simple techniques that can equip a child with acute awareness. And just as we repeat to children the need for manners on a regular basis, so too, we need to follow up and reinforce the teachings of physical boundaries on a regular basis. So I encourage you to take notes so that you can repeat these techniques as you see a need for them.

II.   Why is prevention important?

We know the horrific statistics on sexual abuse of children. Here are some facts and figures from the

United States. One in four females is molested in childhood. One in seven boys is molested before the age of 18. 150,000 to 200,000 new cases of sexual abuse are being reported each year. In England a quarter of all rape victims are children.

In South Africa the largest group of perpetrators (33%) was school teachers. The findings suggest that child rape is becoming more common, and lend support to qualitative research of sexual harassment of female students in schools in Africa. South Africa has one of the highest rates of rape in the world, mostly against children. Every half an hour, a child is sexually abused in Brazil. Sometimes by Brazilians, sometimes by foreigners, who are presented the children by an intermediary who has rented them by the day from their families.

Regarding sexual violence against children in Eastern Europe, Sexual violence against young boys and girls up to 15 years old accounts for 30 per cent of all crimes in this category, and it is most often children between 8 and 12 years old who are attacked. The perpetrators are known to their victims in 50 per cent of cases, and roughly 40 per cent of crimes of this kind are committed by relatives. The enormity of the problem can be realized by the fact that in India alone, at least 25 percent of the adult population has been molested before the age of 16. At least 27 million females are adult survivors of child sexual abuse. In Thailand it is estimated that up to 300,000 children have been sold into sexual slavery. It is a multi-national, multi-billion dollar industry in cities like Pattaya, where the population is 100,000 and 20% are known to be male and female prostitutes, many of them children.[42] These are but samples of a world wide problem that should have all of us working on it. The sexual abuse of children is everyone's business and we must be about how to remedy it.[43]

We also know that immoral, degenerate or ignorant people prey upon the fact that children and their caregivers are not aware. Perpetrators seek out the compliant child. Sadly, some of our youth are acting out the immorality that they have been taught. Power over one's body and path in life starts with knowledge. Remarkably, the moral education of children can start very young. Not only does it include teaching children virtues such as kindness, compassion, love, understanding and friendship, but it includes knowledge of personal boundaries.

The workshop entitled "Protective Behaviors for Children" is a one hour *preventive* workshop that teaches children how to be aware of boundaries for the private areas of their bodies *before* someone does something that is inappropriate or harmful. The program incorporates all of the senses, the different

---

[43] These statistics were taken from the Internet. Simply go to Google and explore by putting in (Country) and the words "child sexual abuse."

ways of knowing, plus the power of speech to help children fully retain what is learned.

Participants in this workshop will learn how to teach children to ask for help, who to ask, how to conquer their fears and how to say NO, STOP, and HELP! They will learn to be aware of three different types of touch: Gentle touch, hurting touch and secret touch. Moreover, this is a vital language skill for the morally educated child. For how else would they be able to define or describe what has happened?

One of the most instinctive virtues a child, even a baby, has is empathy. Perpetrators prey upon this and prey upon the unaware, compliant child. What you can do is teach children to not be compliant in specific situations.

There is a simple song everyone will learn, plus arts and crafts such as the "Fear-A-Lizer" with which they learn to pulverize their fears. They can make a Magic Warrior Shield (made from a simple paper plate or the handout pattern at the back of this paper) that reinforces where internal and external confidence comes from. (*Internal* being the special strengths each individual child has and *external* referring to the system of support that surrounds the child — parents, village mentors, counselors, professionals, etc.) There are two coloring sheets and an outline that will be provided for each participant in this workshop so that attendees such as children, parents, grandparents, babysitters, teachers, therapists, counselors and trainers can have tools to take home with them enabling them to demonstrate the program in their own locality. There is no cost for these tools.

The Protective Behaviors for Children workshop has been presented to schools, orphanages, and Catholic Social Service Agencies in Thailand as well as in Japan, China and the United States. Staff training has also been conducted so that teachers can follow up 3 months or so later.

III. When my grandson, Tanner, was 3 years old, he asked my daughter-in-law, "Who made all the people in the world?" She answered, "God (or a Supreme Being)." Then he asked, "But who made all the bad people?" She answered, "God made all the people and allowed them to make choices, but some people chose to do bad things." A Great Educator that has taught me said that "The root cause of wrong doing is ignorance." So we have a need to educate both the wrong doer for the protection of society and to educate those who are innocent. The following is one method of teaching children to be aware of boundaries.

1. Opening: What children will learn:
   a. How to ask for help
   b. Who to ask for help
   c. How to conquer their fears
   d. That they have permission to say NO! STOP! And HELP!

2. There are three kinds of touch: Gentle touch, hurting touch and secret touch. Describe them. Pat yourself on the arm or cheek very gently to demonstrate gentle touch; pinch yourself and say "OUCH!"to illustrate hurting touch. You can also use a doll or a stuffed animal to give the children a visual image of gentle touch, rocking the doll or stuffed animal. You can also speak of bullies at school or in the neighborhood and the types of behaviors that they exhibit, such as hitting, kicking, punching, twisting arms, and other types of fighting

3. Ask them: "Where are your private places?" And then tell them, "Anywhere you can cross your arms on your body. No one is allowed to do hurting touch or secret touch there. Secret touch is when someone tries to put their hands under your clothing or inside your panties and tells you not to tell Mommy or Daddy (or the authorities)". Talk about people who are trying to do good for them such as a Doctor or a Nurse and differentiate when it is appropriate. Babies and small children, for example, need help with cleaning their private areas and the changing of their diapers. Remember that 80% of cases of sexual abuse are done by family members and therefore the child has to be told that Mommy and Daddy cannot do secret touch, too. Hand out pictures #1 through #4 to demonstrate the following.

a. Face: Have the children (or workshop participant) cross their arms over their face as the boy is doing in picture #1. Talk about the feelings they would have if someone did hurting touch there. Tell them. "No one can touch your face without your permission. Unless they have a good reason to help you." (Don't have them start coloring here yet. Just talk about the pictures and ask them questions about the picture. Ask them what they think the boy is feeling.)

b. Chest: Cross arms over the chest as the girl is doing in picture #2. Talk about the feelings they might have if someone touched them there. Tell them, "No one can touch your chest without your permission." Ask them what they think the girl is feeling.

c. Pelvic area or genitals: Cross arms over their pelvis. Talk about the feelings they perceive on the boy's face in the picture. Tell them, "No one has the right to touch your genitals without your permission." (We will discuss later on what they can say verbally. Because we are an international group and because the children you will teach are at different developmental stages, know that you must choose wording that is familiar to their experience and your locality. You don't have to be limited to this language. You can be creative.)

d. Buttocks: Have them cross their arms over their buttocks. Again, talk about the feelings the little girl in the picture might have or they might have. If you have a mixed group of boys and girls, don't forget to address this issue with the boys, even though there is a girl in picture #4. So it is with all of the pictures.

A word on "Feelings"…children can be taught at a very young age to express their feelings. Feeling language can be very difficult even for adults. To give you an example, I was present when my niece came screaming into a room where all the family was gathered for a holiday. We did not know what was wrong, but my sister held her and said, "Tell Momma, I'm frightened of the helicopter! Tell Momma, I'm frightened." She was teaching her feeling language at 2 and ½ years old. It's as necessary as teaching a child manners and boundaries. The words for feelings in English are on the coloring sheet and there are lines for which the children can write out their own feelings in their own language.

4. Song: This is My Private Place. If you are a musical person and like to sing, make up your own tune to the following words. And if you are not a musical person, just teach them to recite the words like a chant, a nursery rhyme or a poem. I will sing it for you:

> This is my private place. (Cross arms over the face.)
>
> This is my private place. (Cross arms over the chest.)
>
> This is my private place. (Cross arms over the pelvis.)
>
> One, Two, Three, and Four!
>
> When you say "one", demonstrate by crossing arms over the face.
>
> When you say "two", demonstrate by crossing arms over the chest.
>
> When you say "three", demonstrate by crossing arms over the pelvis.
>
> Then quickly turn around and slap both hands on your buttocks saying,
>
> "And four!"

After you have demonstrated it for them two or three times, have them stand up and sing it, going through the motions. You are, in fact, teaching them through movement, motion, music, speech and visualization.

5. Now, hand out the coloring crayons or markers and have them color the pictures. This will be the third or fourth time you have gone through these concepts with them which will help fix it in their memories. Walk around the room from table to table or desk to desk and encourage them and review the information as you acknowledge each one of them individually. Say things like:

What a good job you are doing.

I like the way you color.

Can you tell what feelings are in his or her heart by the expression on the face?

You have a special way of coloring.

What's your favorite color?

Do you like to color at home and at school?

(Translate what feeling words are written in English for each picture. If they can write, have them write the feeling words in Chinese, Thai, Japanese, German, Indian, the African languages, etc.)

6. Ask the children "Have you ever felt embarrassed, afraid or ashamed? Did your stomach hurt?" "What are your favorite foods?" "What foods make you feel sick in your stomach?" "That sick feeling can be called a yuckie feeling. Secret touch can make you feel many different types of feelings which are like warning signs." "If you feel yuckie, uncomfortable or ashamed when someone does secret touch, it's not because of something you did, but because of what THEY did. What I want you to do is run away as fast as you can. That yuckie feeling is a RED FLAG that tells you something is not right and you need to run to someone who is safe and tell them what happened. You can also tell the person who is making you feel uncomfortable 'NO! Stop that! I don't like it when you do that!'"[44] Next we will learn how to teach them to ask for help and who to ask for help if they couldn't run away.

7. Hand out the picture of the hand and the pencils. If you do not have the picture of the hand, you can make one by simply placing

[44] This phrase was adapted from Sandy Kleven, LCSW, The Right Touch, Illumination Arts Publishing Company, Inc. Bellevue, Washington. This is a read-aloud story to help prevent child sexual abuse.

your hand on a blank sheet of paper and tracing around your fingers and your thumb and making copies. Or have the children trace around their own hands on a blank piece of paper. There is a sample provided with this paper.

Have them write NO! STOP! And HELP in large letters or characters in the palm of the hand or write it for them if they are too young, teaching them what the words mean. Have safe scissors ready. Tell the children "To stop hurting touch and secret touch you have to be able to tell someone who is safe, someone you can trust, someone who would only do something good for you and to you." Then ask them "Who is a safe person? Who would you ask to help you? Who would listen to you and believe you?"

Start with the thumb and have them write in a name of someone who is safe...Mom or Dad, for instance. If it is Mom or Dad who is perpetrating the abuse, ask for another name. Go on to the pointer finger (the first finger) and ask them who else can they think of that is safe who would never do secret touch or hurting touch. Have them write in the name of whoever they can think of. They may say Auntie, Grandmother. Move on to the second finger and ask again. If they are having difficulty thinking up people, make suggestions such as brother, cousin, friend. Do the same with the third and fourth fingers, suggesting Doctor, policeman, nurse, or teacher. One boy in an orphanage in Thailand said he would call in the army!

If Mother is listed on a finger, have them say, "Mother, someone is doing secret touch right here!" If Grandfather is on the list, tell them to say, "Grandfather, someone is doing secret touch right here."

Have them color the hand red and cut it out with safe scissors. Red is a universal color for STOP! Have them raise their paper hands together and shout out as a group "NO! STOP! HELP!" Raising the hand is also a universal sign for HELP!

If you are in a class room situation, all the hands of the children can be placed on a bulletin board to remind them of this exercise. Attention can be drawn to the bulletin board after a two week period has passed and the techniques can be reviewed.

Then tell them, "If the person on the thumb doesn't listen, tell the person on the pointer finger. If that person doesn't listen, tell the person on the next finger, and the next, and keep telling until someone listens. Don't stop! Be brave! Be courageous! Keep telling and telling and telling and don't stop until someone listens!"

8. Skills and Tools:

Bravery and courage come from having skills and tools. Children become fearful and compliant because they are either unaware of what is happening or they don't know what to do. The equipment you will need for this part of the workshop are crackers, plastic bags, scotch tape, markers and a rolling pin or other long round object (like a tall glass or a long 1 inch wooden dowel) that can crush the cracker that is in the plastic bag. The following list of skills should be written on slips of paper. Each child will tape the skills to the rolling pin or tall glass or even a piece of wood. Be creative. Have at least three or four different slips of paper for each child.

    a. I know what hurting touch and secret touch are.
    b. I can run away as fast as I can
    c. I can yell for help and say NO! STOP! And Help!
    d. I'm a quick thinker!
    e. I'm a smart and brave kid.
    f. I know ahead of time who to ask for help!
    g. I can tell 5 people and keep telling until someone listens.

h. I can say "Stop that! I don't like it when you do that!"
i. I know my body belongs to me and nobody can touch it.

After all of the children have read their skills aloud, tape them with the scotch tape to the rolling pin or cylindrical object. Then hand out the crackers, plastic bags and wide-tip Sanford Markers. Have them write FEAR on the cracker and put the cracker in the plastic bag, sealing it shut. Now one at a time, have them crush their fear with their powerful skills that are taped to the rolling pin, telling them "Look how strong you are! You know what to say and do! Good for you! You can conquer your fears because you have special powers." Say the verbal skills out loud again to all of them. These skills give them powers. Tell them that they can take their plastic bags home with them, open them when they are outside and let the wind blow all the cracker crumbs away, releasing their fears. Be sure to have extra crackers so that the children can have a treat to celebrate this moment. Do warn them not to eat the cracker that they have written on with the marker because it has chemicals on it.

9. Every country has its Warriors! The next craft project you will teach the children to make is a Magic Warrior Shield. The pattern

for it is attached to the back of this paper. You should copy it onto card stock or card board that is thin enough to cut out with scissors. The strip on the bottom is to be stapled to the back so they can slip their hand into it and hold it in front of themselves as a Magic Warrior Shield. (You could also use paper plates if they are available in your country.) Hand out pencils, markers and a stapler or two.

a. Have them draw a picture on the Shield of someone who would protect them, such as parents, the family dog, a policewoman or a doctor. One child asked me to draw an attack cat on hers! This is their outside help (external guidance).

b. Tell them to write NO! STOP! HELP! On the inside of the Shield. This is their personal, inside strength.

c. If there are any of the SKILLS left over from the previous project, have them tape some to the inside. Discuss these skills out loud as they work, telling them that they have the personal power of a Warrior.

d. When they are finished creating their Magic Warrior Shields, have them hold them up in front of themselves as if they are brave, courageous and strong with a Shield of skills and helpers to protect them. Then have them, as a group, say, "NO! STOP! HELP!" again.

10. There are three more important points to teach the children.

    a. They have to tell one of the five people on their hand even if the person doing the secret touch says they will harm someone the child loves. Sex offenders count on the fear of the child as their ally. They count on the child being unaware and powerless. This workshop teaches children what to do ahead of time. This is prevention before it happens, before the abuse is buried, so that the child will have the opportunity to talk things out.

    b. The children must be taught that if someone does secret touch, it is not the fault of the child. Some children think that it is their fault and that may keep them from saying something out loud. So tell them over and over throughout the work shop, "It would not be your fault."

    c. The final concept to bring before them is this: "Nothing that can happen to you is so terrible that you can't say it out loud to someone you trust." Have them say it out loud to you, too.

"Nothing that can happen to me is so terrible that I can't say it out loud to someone I trust."

11. Now, have them stand up and repeat the song: "This is my Private Place!

> This is my private place! (Cross arms over face.)
>
> This is my private place! (Cross arms over chest.)
>
> This is my private place! (Cross arms over pelvis.)
>
> One, two, three, and four!
>
> (On one cross arms over face, on two cross arms over chest, on three cross arms over pelvis, and on four turn your back to them and slap your hands on your buttocks.)

Free Handouts for this program can be found at www.skylarkpubl.com

in English, Spanish and French under the title of Free Materials.

IV. Closing

In the book, "The Right Touch", author Sandy Kleven makes several very good suggestions on how to get help for the child and how to rectify the situation. If a child comes to you and tells you that someone has touched them inappropriately, BELIEVE THE CHILD! Give the child plenty of reassurance that it was right to tell and that it was not his or her fault. Remember that you are not qualified to confront the accused offender, so you must turn it over to the authorities. You can request assistance from the police, sheriff, or a child protection agency.

I know that we have many countries represented here today, so I couldn't begin to know the many agencies that are and are not available to you. I can give you an example from the United States. There is a Childhelp USA Hotline at 1-800-4-A-Child that has trained counselors available 24 hours a day for crisis intervention. They can also offer referrals to counseling agencies and support groups. They offer literature upon request. Children and adults may be connected to counselors in 144 languages as needed.

Ms. Kleven says you can also use the Internet to find a vast network of resources to help deal with this unfortunate but all-too-common problem that is an epidemic world wide. The Childhelp USA site is a good place to start: www.childhelpusa.org or you can e-mail them at help@childhelpusa.org.[45]   In Africa you can access www.lifeline.org

What else can you do? You can recognize that this is a community problem as well as a world wide problem, not an individual problem. You can start a support group with the women and men in your community, teaching this work shop on a regular basis in order to empower both the children and the adults. Adult mothers who have not received counseling for their own abuse are known to not have good boundaries and skills and awareness to prevent this injustice happening to their own children.

If we go back to the statistics, say in India alone where at least 27 million adult females have experienced child sexual abuse, imagine the percentage that don't have good boundaries or awareness to protect their own children so it becomes a generational problem that could have been prevented with education for sustainable development.

When I was teaching protective behaviors in Thailand to a group of teachers, a woman approached me after my talk. She said that a four year neighbor boy had forced her 2 year old grand daughter into the oral sex position on his body. She

---

[45] Sandy Kleven, "The Right Touch", © 1997, Illumination Arts Publishing Company, Inc., Bellevue, Washington.

didn't know what to do. She was afraid of offending his father who was a well respected man in town. Yet she did not know how to interpret the boy's behavior...if it was something he had seen in the home, she couldn't be sure...but she felt a great need to protect her grand daughter.

I told her it was time for her to rise up to leadership in her community and act as though this was a community problem not an individual problem. She could gather the adults and children in her community to teach them the concepts in this workshop to create awareness as a preventive measure and continue to teach her grand child through the years to protect her. That way she would not have to point a finger at any individual, but enlighten the entire community.

At one time I was at a conference in New York City when a woman revealed to me that she allowed a trusted male friend to baby-sit her 6 year old daughter while she attended a meeting. Her husband was out of town. When she returned home and her friend, a member of her church, had left, she started putting her daughter to bed. It was then that her daughter said, "I hope Mr. Smith never touches me again like he did tonight."

Her mother's heart was in her throat! But she remained calm. "Where did Mr. Smith touch you?" The little girl said, "Right here," pointing to her pubic area. The first thing her mother did was believe her child. Then she said, "How did it make you feel?" The little girl said, "Yuckie!" Her mother asked her, "Do you want to talk about it?" The little girl said, "No, not right now, I just want to go to bed." "Well," said her mother, "If you want to talk about it later, I have a special friend who is really good about talking about such things and we'll go and see her. But I want you to know that it wasn't your fault that Mr. Smith did that and you will never have to be alone with him again."

Then she tucked her daughter in bed and went to her room and screamed into her pillow. The next morning she called Mr. Smith. Fortunately she had recently learned how to create an I-Statement, so she formed her words very carefully to that format.

And she said, "Mr. Smith, I want you to know that I feel very angry that you touched my daughter in an inappropriate way and I want to know what you plan to do so that you will never touch another child in this way and so that you will stop losing friends and to correct your behavior in the future? I know that you were to come to my house for a meeting this weekend, but you are no longer welcome in my home. You are never to see my daughter again because I think that would be detrimental to her healing." Mr. Smith stumbled over his words, said as he wept that he was sorry and that he would get some help.[46]

Today that little girl is about 16 to 18 years old and is whole and healthy because she felt safe enough to communicate this out loud to her mother and the incident wasn't buried without discussion and support. She was told that it was not her fault and she was protected from ever being alone with this man again. Imagine though, if her mother had been able to follow up and teach her the skills in this workshop, to reinforce these concepts.

Here is one last story and then I will open the program up to questions and discussion. I may not be able to answer all the questions, but together as a group I am sure we will find suggestions and solutions that will expand our knowledge on this very important subject.

A more subtle but dangerous form of abuse:

One year when I was traveling from city to city in Wisconsin, my hostess in one home greeted me at the door. Her three year old daughter was at her side. Susan, a former social worker, explained to me that Frances did not like to be hugged or touched. I was very impressed with the fact that this mother was immediately setting boundaries for me in order to support her daughter's feelings and

---

[46] Phyllis Peterson, Assisting the Traumatized Soul, © 1999, Baha'i Publishing Trust, Wilmette, IL, p. 133

preferences. I always make a point of allowing a child to come to me rather than me forcing myself onto a child. Children sense who is to be trusted and if left to themselves will test the water so to speak.

I was there to demonstrate my "Boundary Sculpting Game" which creates consciousness of what we do unconsciously instead of setting clear boundaries with others. Susan invited many of her neighbors and there were plenty of people participating in the game. After the game I provided time for discussion and memories of times we had either crossed the boundaries of others or they had crossed our boundaries.

Susan revealed an interesting problem that was confronting her at family holiday gatherings. Her family knew was Frances' preferences were, yet Susan's brother would tease and cajole Frances to hug him even though she consistently told him "No!" Then he would make a game out of it, trying to turn her NO into a YES! He would work away at her until finally she acquiesced. Then the entire family would laugh.

Susan would be very disturbed but did not have support in putting her brother in his place, at a safe distance from Frances. She was also afraid of rocking the boat and ruining family gatherings by setting rigid boundaries, or being thought of as rigid.

What was really happening was this: In Susan's brother's eyes, Frances' no did not mean NO!

Now, many of us who work with youth, teenagers and women who have been raped on dates, know that their NO did not mean NO to the rapist. Susan's daughter was in a precarious situation in the developmental years of her life. And after playing "The Boundary Sculpting Game", Susan had finally found the key, the language, and the concepts to verbalize what was actually going on within this situation.

Through the group discussion that we had, Susan decided that she had to firmly tell her brother "No!" and that if he did not respond appropriately to her authority as Frances' mother, then she would not attend family gatherings until he did.

Remember, the greatest need with Protective Behaviors for Children is to empower them with knowledge of how to say NO and to support them with awareness of boundaries for the private areas of their bodies. Next they need the skills for asking for help. They need to be told that it was not their fault. And if upon hearing that the child has been abused, the child must be assured that they are believed. Ask questions about their feelings, teach them the feeling language. There are over 250 feeling words in the English language. Use every opportunity to help children to express their feelings from the youngest age possible. And please also remember that you must turn it over to qualified authorities when someone has done something to break the law. There are laws against child sexual abuse and you may not have the authority to confront the individual or enforce the law. And so I finish the program with these final words that can be said to the child:

There is nothing that can happen to you that is so terrible that you can't say it out loud to someone you trust.

Thank you for coming today and thank you so much for caring.

Questions and Discussion.

Handouts attached. ***Excerpts from "Assisting the Traumatized Soul" used by permission of the National Spiritual Assembly of the Baha'is of the United States.

Protective Behavior Tools

These statements are to be cut into strips and placed in a box for the participants to take out. Copy this page in order to keep it as a master. If you have more than 9 children, make another set. They will tape it onto a rolling pin to crush a cracker that has "Fear" written on it. Place the cracker in a plastic sandwich bag. The statement is their personal power, "knowledge" that can crush their fear.

a. I know what hurting touch and secret touch are.

b. I can run away as fast as I can.

c. I can yell HELP and say NO! STOP!

d. I'm a quick thinker!

e. I'm a smart and brave kid.

f. I know ahead of time who to ask for help!

g. I can tell 5 people and keep telling until someone listens.

h. I can say "Stop that! I don't like it when you do that!"

i. I know my body belongs to me and nobody can touch it.

Protective Behaviors for Children Outline

1. Opening: What you will learn:
   a. How to ask for help
   b. Who to ask for help
   c. How to conquer your fears
   d. How to say "No!"

2. Describe the three kinds of touch: Gentle, hurting, and secret touch. Use a doll or stuffed animal to demonstrate. Pat the stuffed toy or baby doll gently to show how we must treat children. Tell them that is gentle touch. Ask the children if they've ever been pinched or hit. Tell them that is Hurting touch.

3. Secret touch is done to your private places. Where are your private places? (some children will know.) Anywhere you can cross your arms on your body. No one is allowed to do hurting touch or secret touch there. What about the Doctor or someone who is trying to do good for you?

   a. Give them pictures #1 through #4.

b. Face – Have them cross their arms over their face. Talk about the feelings the boy is showing on his face in picture #1. Write them down in the blank spaces. The child can write the feelings in their own language.

c. Chest – Cross arms over their chest. Talk about the feelings the little girl in picture #2 is showing on her face. Write the feelings down.

d. Pelvic area or genitals. – Cross arms over their pelvis. Talk about the feelings the boy is showing in the picture #3. Write them down.

e. Buttocks – Cross arms over their buttocks. Talk about the feelings in picture # 4.

4. Demonstrate the song: "This is my private place!" Then have them stand up and sing it three times.

This is my private place (cross hands over face).
This is my private place (cross hands over chest.)
This is my private place (cross hands over pelvis.)
ONE! (face)
TWO! (Chest)

THREE! (Pelvis)
AND (Turn around)
FOUR! (Slap your backside on four)

5. Hand out the markers or crayons. Now let them color the pictures. Encourage them and review as you walk around the tables. Say things such as:

What a good job you are doing.

I like the way you color.

Can you tell what feelings are in his or her heart by the expression on the face?

You have a special way of coloring.

What's your favorite color?

Do you like to color at home and at school?

6. Tell me what its like when you feel embarrassed or ashamed or Yuckie. (Pause and wait for answers. Acknowledge their embarrassment.) If you feel ashamed when someone does secret touch, its not because of something you did but because of what the other person did. They should feel ashamed.

7. Hand out the picture of the hand and the pencils. Have them write "NO!" "STOP!" and "HELP!" in large letters in the palm of the hand. Tell them that the hand is a universal symbol for "NO! STOP! And HELP. Have them yell know as a group as loud as they can! (Tell them that wasn't loud enough and tell them to yell "NO!" again. They'll get the idea and you will have a better result.) Do the same with "STOP! And "HELP!" Have safe scissors ready.

8. To stop hurting touch and secret touch, you have to be able to tell someone who is safe, someone you can trust, someone who would only do something good for you and to you. Who is safe? Start with the thumb and write in a name of someone who is safe. Raise your hand and tell me who is safe! (You'll get a variety of answers. Write them on the board.) Mom, Dad, Auntie, Grandma, brother, cousin, friend, Doctor, Policeman, Nurse, Teacher. Write one of these names on each finger and thumb. Cut out the hand.

9. Tell the person on the thumb. If the person on the thumb doesn't listen, tell the pointer finger. If that person doesn't listen, tell the

next, and keep telling until someone listens. Don't stop! Be brave!

10. Color the hand red, which Is also a universal symbol for stop. And cut out the hand. Have everyone raise their red hand in the air and on cue yell, "NO!   STOP! HELP!"

11. Did you know that bravery and courage come from having skills, tools and knowing what to do ahead of time? Children become fearful because they don't know what to do and they are afraid to speak up. Here are some tools you can use:

    a. I know what hurting touch and secret touch are.

    b. I can run away as fast as I can

    c. I can yell for help and say NO! STOP! And Help!

    d. I'm a quick thinker!

    e. I'm a smart and brave kid.

f. I know ahead of time who to ask for help!

g. I can tell 5 people and keep telling until someone listens.

h. I can say "Stop that! I don't like it when you do that!"

i. I know my body belongs to me and nobody can touch it.

12. Conquering Fear with the Fear-a-Lizer! (a Rolling Pin, a tall glass)
    a. Hand out the crackers, small plastic bags, scotch tape and markers.
    b. Write FEAR on the Cracker (other countries may call it a biscuit..
    c. Place the cracker in the bag.
    d. Tape your skills and tools on the rolling pin.
    e. Now crush your fears with the powerful skills and the fear-a-lizer.
13. Hand out the paper plates, pencils, markers and staplers and talk about the Magic Power Shield used by the Plains Indians to illustrate inside and outside power.

a. Draw a picture on the paper plate of someone who will protect you. Parents, family dog, Policeman, counselor.
b. Write HELP, STOP, and NO and the #5 (5 people remember who will be safe and protect you?)
c. Write down the name of the person on the front of the plate.
d. Tape some of the skills on the inside.
e. Staple the cardboard strip to the sides of the plate and everyone hold their plate up to talk about it.

14. Closing: What have we learned today? Ask them to raise their hands and say what they have learned.
a. AND, tell them, "Nothing that can happen to you is so terrible that you can't say it out loud to someone you trust!" Say it again, "Nothing that can happen to you is so terrible that you can't say it out loud to someone you trust."

SONG: This is my Private Place! (Sing it three times.)

Thank the children and parents for coming today! If this class has been conducted in a school room, they can put all the hands on the bulletin board as a reminder of what they have learned and for the teacher to review the points.

Chapter Ten, brings home the necessity for women to achieve detachment. May you be successful in attracting God's bounty for you to declare and gain human rights for yourself and your daughters and your sons.

Chapter Ten

The Meaning of Detachment For Women

You have asked me to help you understand the meaning of detachment and this missive is to try to clarify the subject in my own mind and heart. I don't know if this is how the major Figures of our Faith would express the subject, but it seems important to try to interpret the prayers for detachment in the light of the issues that beleaguer even the most deepened Bahá'ís right now at the turn of this Century.

One of the things that I have noticed about the prayers that Bahá'u'lláh and 'Abdu'l-Bahá have revealed for women is that there is usually a reference to "detachment" embedded within them. I have often wondered why that is the case, and I have concluded that it must be because God understands the plight of women. All of the virtues are choices. Love is a choice. We also choose justice and truthfulness. But detachment is sometimes vague and conflicting.

If women have more difficulty with detachment, I believe it could be because "choice" has been prohibited for women. Once we make a choice, then we have fear because we know there are consequences for choices, short term and long term. Every woman who enters into a sexual relationship with a man knows this fear. It strikes at the core of her being, unless she is preparing for motherhood. Choice carries responsibility as well as blame. Women fear blame because culturally women have been blamed throughout history. We also fear detachment because it implies that we do not care and that we are not responsive as human beings. Women have been trained to care and respond instantly and to believe that there is something inherently wrong with them if they do not care and respond cart blanch.

Turning to the prayers for detachment in Bahá'í Prayers, especially the last one that was written expressly for the handmaidens of God, we see that 'Abdu'l-Bahá prescribes that women be detached from all things. "O God, my God! Fill up for me the cup of detachment from all things, and in the assembly of Thy splendors and bestowals, rejoice me with the wine of loving Thee." Being detached from all things is kind of nebulous, so I am going to try to be very specific. He further uses phrases like "free me from" and "break off from me", and "grant that I may die to all that I possess."[47] Another word that is a key to detachment is "sanctify" which means to

---

[47] All quotations by 'Abdu'l-Baha in this passage are from Baha'i Prayers, c 2002, /BPT, p. 57-58

make ourselves, our desires holy, which we cannot do unless we detach ourselves from that which is not holy.

Bahá'u'lláh refers to Christ as the "Essence of Detachment" in the Kitab-i-Iqan when He said "Let the dead bury the dead. He also refers to all the Manifestations of God as "Tabernacles of Holiness"[48], showing us that there is a definite process by which we are to detach ourselves from the world in order to achieve holiness..

The Twelve Step programs have a familiar phrase that we can draw on to explain detachment: "Let go and let God." And here's a story that children enjoy about a monkey who wanted a piece of fruit that was inside a hole in a tree. His hand could just barely fit inside the hole and once grasping the fruit, he could no longer withdraw his hand. Yet he wanted the fruit so badly that even though he was in great danger he clung tightly to it. Instead of escaping from an animal that was in pursuit of him, he was captured and eaten. All he would have had to do was let go of the fruit. His hand would be "free" from what he wanted to possess and he would have been able to escape the danger.

So, too, we need to be free from our desires, be detached from them, in order to let God work wonders in our lives. We have just finished the Fast,

---

[48] Gleanings from the Writings of Baha'u'llah, BPT, p. 47

one of the purposes of which is to teach us about detachment. Bahá'u'lláh teaches us to "hold" to His Name and "cling" to His hem. "Thou seest me, O my God, holding to Thy Name, the Most Holy, the Most Luminous, the Most Mighty, the Most Great, the Most Exalted, the Most Glorious, and clinging to the hem of the robe to which have clung all in this world and in the world to come." BP, p. 238-239. If we want to "drink the cup of detachment from all things", we need to examine a few of the things that we are holding onto and clinging to.

Since I am the author of "Assisting the Traumatized Soul: Healing the Wounded Talisman", I believe I should first state that we must be detached from our own "authority" . It seems obvious that because we are fallible and must seek a higher authority all of our lives, that all of our powers must be subject to the Will of God, the Authority of God. This would include, of course, our will and the other 30 powers.

We know that we each have a unique perspective with resulting opinions and viewpoints about life, the behavior of others, the decisions our friends, children, spouse, parents, or local Spiritual Assemblies make, and our own experiences; but these, too, we must be detached from, for as Abdu'l-Bahá states, we may be worshipping "an error of perception."[49] When we come to the point where we recognize comfortably that there are "multiple-

---

[49] Selections from the Writings of 'Abdu'l-Baha, BPT, p. 53

perspectives", each of them valid, then we will be at the point where we can be released from error and find "truth" or "certitude."

We must be detached from consultation and remember that there are many different types and degrees of consultation. The highest form is a spiritual consultation with our institutions of Authority on earth, as well as consultation with a recognized, trusted professional. The lowest form would be "consulting" with those who have a private interest in the results or the outcome.

We must be detached from blame, too, whether it is the blame that someone is trying to attach to us or the blame we are trying to attach to others. We live in a culture that assigns blame to mothers and to women in general. So that if we are a woman who has not been offered or sought equality, we are likely to accept this blame without question. We must also recognize that when we are blaming others or ourselves, we are participating in an unhealthy aspect of our culture--using old world order behavior in our precious Bahá'í community.

We need to be detached from passion and desire. Another way of stating detachment from passion is this: We need to be detached from emotional reasoning, because emotional reasoning fuels our passion and desire. Our emotions are a power that is meant to give us information about how we feel about what we are doing or what is happening to us.

We then transfer this information to other powers such as our reasoning power which includes inductive and deductive reasoning. If our emotions are negative and indeed false depending upon the situation, then the result of our reasoning is going to be detrimental to our mental and emotional well-being. We will draw wrong conclusions about people as well as God. It seems to me that "superiority" must be emotional reasoning about our abilities or presumed rights because it leads to an emotional high about our presumed "station," as well as "justification of anger and prejudice" against others, anger being another emotion we reason with. Reasoning must be based on facts, scientific knowledge, the Word of God and the Covenant of Bahá'u'lláh. This does not preclude using the power of "intuition" as a means of establishing certitude.

As Bahá'ís who want to teach others about the Faith, we must also be detached from the results of our teaching. This does not mean that we will not be concerned about improving our methods of teaching, but that we will not become disheartened that others do not respond right away, whether it is our spouse, our children, our neighbors or friends. Certainly we must pray for them, but trust that God is working toward their good in ways that we may never know.

As parents, we must be detached from the character development of our children. This does not mean that we will not be involved in their character development. We are most definitely responsible for teaching them the Word of God, the importance of obedience to a higher authority, the development of virtues, and the vital necessity of unity, cooperation and reciprocity. However, they are fully responsible for the development of their character all throughout their lives, as we are for our own. This does not mean that we do not continue to pray and attempt to guide. Detachment from the path a child takes would be the greatest difficulty for mothers especially. Women are criticized for not meeting the expectations of onlookers who always seem to know best what to do and fall into the trap of blaming mothers. Women are expected to be "attached" to others' expectations. Women are expected to be attached to relationships that fail and the failure of children in school..

Those of us who have had a troubled childhood desire to be detached from shame. We also desire to be detached from the memory of abuse, the rehearsing of abuse issues, and the very figure that abused us. It is difficult if an adult has never spoken out loud that they have internalized shame about sexual abuse, verbal abuse, physical abuse, as well as having lived with parents who have been addicted to alcohol or other drugs. The only way that I know to become detached from the shame of others, which I have owned, is to externalize it verbally and have it validated, as well as pour it out in prayer to Bahá'u'lláh. When we have been "locked" into a perspective of shame for decades, we need to hear multiple viewpoints on this topic that will invalidate our ownership of this injustice. Turning to the Writings we find that Abdu'l-Bahá comforts us with this quotation from Fire and Gold, "Thy letter was received. Thou has written: 'I am not worthy.' Who is worthier than thee? Hadst thou not been worthy, thou wouldst not have turned to God and wouldst not have wished to enter the Kingdom. Thy worthiness has guided thee until this blessing and bounty have encompassed thee."[50] Those who are recovering from abuse need to feel that worthiness. And there's a clue! Worthiness obliterates blame and thereby increases our ability to detach from our propensity to cling to our memories of abuse and our abuser. Our inherent worthiness and nobility have guided us from our early experience of degradation to knowledge, understanding and detachment from that experience.

Here's another thought: We need to be detached from our weakness and frailty. Speaking for myself, I take medication that is necessary for my mental stability. I feel that is a weakness because I do not like to take medication. Nor do I like to admit that under stress my mental balance is at risk without medication. Either I feel shame about that or I detach myself from that shame and refuse to own the stigmatism that is prevalent in our culture. Everybody has a weakness. What difference does it

---

[50] 'Abdu'l-Baha, Fire and Gold, Compiled by Brian Kurzius, George Ronald, © 1995, p. 212

make if it is a weakness in the colon or a propensity for migraine headaches or varicose veins? Is it better to have a weakness of body or a weakness of character? And for those of us who believe they have a weakness of character, the above quotation on "worthiness" is meant to support them, too. All of us have weakness of character. That's why there are prayers for steadfastness, forgiveness, protection and assistance with tests. Bahá'u'lláh quotes a poet, "Even or odd, thou shalt win the wager"[51], if we are keepers of His Covenant. I believe that this relates to mental and physical disabilities as well as weakness of character. There are those in the history of the Faith who had such physical disabilities that they had to be carried on a gurney to teach the Faith. So we are told to not heed our weakness and frailties, to be detached from them.

It is obvious that we must be detached from materialism and the comforts that come with it. We are lured by our culture and the media that drives it to live as comfortably as we can possibly live. But tragically, what goes wanting is justice for those who are poverty stricken. And poverty is driven by racism and sexism and the numbers of African American men and women in prison, whose families are

---

[51] Sa'di, Muslihu'd-Din of Shiraz (d. AH 691/AD 1291), famed author of the "Gulistan" and other poetical works. Compilation of Compilations, Vol. I, p. 154
41 Gleanings from the Writings of Baha'u'llah, p. 328-329

destitute and destroyed by their imprisonment. So in order to strive toward greater and greater equity for those who are destitute we need to be detached from materialism and comfort. But Bahá'u'lláh tells us, "O My servants! Sorrow not if, in these days and on this earthly plane, things contrary to your wishes have been ordained and manifested by God, for days of blissful joy, of heavenly delight, are assuredly in store for you. Worlds, holy and spiritually glorious, will be unveiled to your eyes. You are destined by Him, in this world and hereafter, to partake of their benefits, to share in their joys, and to obtain a portion of their sustaining grace. To each and every one of them you will, no doubt, attain."[52]

We must also examine the need to be detached from the ever-present media. It's influence is so overpowering considering that we are bombarded with it from birth. Our characters have been shaped by it unless we were born to parents who had a highly developed power of discernment and who, therefore screened every movie we watched, every book and magazine we read, and every hero we worshipped, instead of using the television as a babysitter. For myself, I absorbed the sexism, racism and materialism in my culture and it contributed to my being dependent, misinformed, ignorant, racist, and a great lover of material comfort. However, I also absorbed Christianity in my culture which laid the foundation for my spiritual growth, investigation into other religions, and eventually led me to Bahá'u'lláh. The greatest protection from the invasive media that surrounds us is turning to the Writings of Bahá'u'lláh, deepening every single day, reciting His Most Glorious Name 95 times each day as well as our obligatory prayer, teaching the Faith daily, and striving through prayer and action to keep His Covenant. This is the meaning of "holding to His Name" and "clinging to the Hem of His Robe."

Bahá'u'lláh offers in Words of Wisdom: "The essence of true safety is to observe silence, to look at the end of things and to renounce the world."[53] The way that I understand this is that we cannot speak safely about faulty philosophies, theologies, and psychologies, unless they are verified by His Revelation. That we are to be detached from them because we cannot possibly have enough wisdom to expound upon all of them. This silence is not imposed upon us to disempower us, but is encouraged because our voice, our power of utterance, is important to the guidance of others. Their future and safety is dependent upon hearing what Bahá'u'lláh has to say about whatever issues they bring to us. Therefore we have a grave responsibility to either speak correctly if we are imbued with knowledge or to observe silence if we do not have wisdom about the subject at hand. If we are not detached from the ignorance in the culture the seeker is trying to escape, we will perpetuate the

---

[53] Tablets of Baha'u'llah, p. 156

ignorance, instead of guiding him or her toward the light. This would illustrate being detached from our power of utterance.

A good example of being detached from faulty psychology would be in such a simple thing as the concept of "low self-esteem." We, of course, want to encourage those who have low self-esteem, but there are now conflicting theories about how we get our self-esteem. We can encourage others, give them praise and acknowledgement around the clock, but they will still leave our Firesides with low self-esteem. This is the way psychology has been for years teaching us to remedy this difficulty.

However, recent studies now prove that men and women develop self-esteem in different ways. For women self-esteem is based on relationship and connection rather than being told that they are "special" and "unique." From this we can make the connection of self-esteem with "unity", a Bahá'í theological concept, instead of "individualism," a western philosophy. The issues the world faces today are filled with nuances like this that conflict greatly with what the Bahá'í teachings really are all about.

Aside from these issues, the very purpose of striving for detachment is God's plan for the unification of the planet, and Bahá'u'lláh's dearest wish for the Oneness of all humankind, as He shows in the Hidden Words: "O CHILDREN OF MEN! Know ye not why We created you all from the same dust?

That no one should exalt himself over the other. Ponder at all times in your hearts how ye were created. Since we have created you all from one same substance it is incumbent on you to be even as one soul, to walk with the same feet, eat with the same mouth and dwell in the same land, that from your inmost being, by your deeds and actions, the signs of oneness and the essence of detachment may be made manifest. Such is my counsel to you, O concourse of light! Heed ye this counsel that ye may obtain the fruit of holiness from the tree of wondrous glory." HW #68 This is proof that in order to prepare for the signs of oneness, we must first develop detachment. It also indicates that detachment prepares us for holiness, and that the fruit of holiness follows detachment.

So, whether you identify with a "let go and let God" philosophy, or the story of the monkey whose hand is caught as he clutches too tightly to the fruit he so desires, or the "detachment from all things" that Bahá'u'lláh wants us to "choose" in order to attain to holiness, these are some ideas to consider.

Chapter Eleven
Thoughts on the Battering and Rape
of Women, Girls, and Boys

In the year 2000 I was travel teaching through northern Michigan when I encountered a Mother who was a Baha'i. She told me about her daughter who was being beaten every day by her husband. She had taught her daughter since childhood that she must be kind. Using the first Arabic Hidden Word by Baha'u'llah, she stressed "O SON OF BEING! My first counsel is this. Possess a pure, kindly, and radiant heart that thine may be a sovereignty ancient, imperishable and everlasting." Her daughter, unfortunately, believed if she was patient and kindly enough, she would eventually have a marriage and relationship that worked. The daughter didn't have the advantage of receiving knowledge that "some" people are tyrants and that showing them kindness only enables them to persist in their behavior as they perceive their victim to be weak and ignorant. "Kindness cannot be shown the tyrant, the deceiver, or the thief, because, far from awakening them to the error of their ways, it maketh them to continue in their perversity as before."
(Abdu'l-Baha, Selections from the Writings of Abdu'l-Baha, p. 158)

We must not only teach the virtues, but teach our children the writings that are designed to protect themselves. This is one reason I created the Protective Behaviors for Children Program...to give children awareness of the language of protection. In the Appendix of this manual you will find two powerful articles from Baha'i Institutions on prevention of violence and sexual abuse of women and girls.[54]

Women's Self-Defense, Level One: Rape Escape

There is a powerful video on Youtube that demonstrates how to escape when someone is attempting to rape you. You can find it at: https://www.youtube.com/watch?v=6D8r-wH0dkk

Steps to prevent Rape:

Learn basic steps you can take to protect yourself. The steps are easy to follow and apply. I'm not implying that there is a solution to a gang rape situation, but again I'm creating awareness.

When out at night, there is safety in numbers. Don't walk alone in the dark or in a parking garage. Wear comfortable shoes so that you can run.

---

[54] Author's note.

The following comes from a website on-line. (http://www.wikihow.com/Prevent-a-Potential-Rape) Rapists are predators. Period. By following these steps, you can try to make your world a little safer from those predators. You will get information and skills you need to protect yourself psychologically and physically. Remember, although being aware of your surroundings and knowing how to defend yourself is important, rape is ultimately the rapist's fault, *not* the victim's. This article is not meant to justify a rapist's actions in any way—it simply provides tips that can help *you* feel safer. In an ideal world, the best way to prevent a potential rape is to educate all members of both sexes to respect and help each other. However, being informed can also go a long way in helping you avoid dangerous situations.

Know that nothing you do will ever make rape your fault. Before you even start thinking about preventing a potential rape, you have to understand that if you are raped, it is 100% the rapist's fault, and that nothing you did, wore, or said could have caused you to be raped. There is no such thing as "asking for it," and anyone who leads you to believe otherwise is deeply misguided. Though you can certainly take measures to improve your chances of avoiding danger and staying safe, in the end, nothing you can do can "cause" you to be raped.

Understand that the best thing that can be done to prevent rape is to prevent people from raping. In today's culture, there are many things that can be done to prevent rape, and it starts with the way women are perceived. If we work, as a society, to raise men who are respectful of women and stop contributing to a culture that objectifies and belittles women constantly, then we can slowly start to turn things around. Sometimes, adolescent boys think "rape jokes" are funny and that it's okay to joke around about sexual assault, and it's important to let them know that this is not the case. Men can also be raped, but society has taken into itself that men "can't possibly be raped", and so most men are ashamed and afraid if they speak out.

- Many people feel that giving women guidelines about things that can be done to stay safe actually shames them and makes them feel like avoiding rape is all about having women act "the right way," and that if they make a misstep, it is basically their fault that they got raped. This is not wikiHow's intention. We intend to empower women by giving them some sensible advice on how to avoid danger. However, women are not the only sex to be raped. Men can be raped, but it just isn't as prevalent. Society doesn't believe "petite little women" can rape "big strong men", and yet it still happens.

Don't ever stop living your life. It can be overwhelming to read the advice about preventing rape. You'll start to feel like there's no place you're safe -- not your grocery store parking lot, not a restroom at a bar, not your car, and not even your own home. You might start to wonder where one can go to be completely safe from rapists. But you can't think like this. Though you should take some precautions, you can't be afraid to leave home by yourself, to be outside late at night, or to go to some of your favorite places. You can still enjoy your life and feel secure without the constant paranoia that you may feel after reading about how to prevent rape.

Drinking Alcohol. "This is a huge red flag for a Baha'i. Baha'u'llah tells us to refrain from drinking alcohol. Not only does it numb the brain, but it incapacitates a person and undermines their power of discernment, their ability to discern right from wrong. I would advise a woman to not drink alcohol, period! This manual is written for the Baha'i and for those who are not Baha'i. The tips that follow about drinking alcohol may be helpful to those who are not Baha'i; but my personal belief is that drinking alcohol is detrimental to the safety both women and men are seeking.

<u>Here is a powerful quotation from Baha'u'llah's Most Holy Book, the Kitab-i-Aqdas.</u>
It is inadmissible that man, who hath been endowed with reason, should consume that which stealeth it away. Nay, rather it behoveth him to comport himself in a manner worthy of the human station, and not in accordance with the misdeeds of every heedless and wavering soul. (Baha'u'llah, The Kitab-i-Aqdas, p. 62)

There are many references in the Bahá'í Writings which prohibit the use of wine and other intoxicating drinks and which describe the deleterious effect of such intoxicants on the individual. In one of His Tablets, Bahá'u'lláh states:

Beware lest ye exchange the Wine of God for your own wine, for it will stupefy your minds, and turn your faces away from the Countenance of God, the All-Glorious, the Peerless, the Inaccessible. Approach it not, for it hath been forbidden unto you by the behest of God, the Exalted, the Almighty.

'Abdu'l-Bahá explains that the Aqdas prohibits "both light and strong drinks", and He states that the reason for prohibiting the use of alcoholic drinks is because "alcohol leadeth the mind astray and causeth the weakening of the body". Shoghi Effendi, in letters written on his behalf, states that this prohibition includes not only the consumption of wine but of "everything that deranges the mind", and he clarifies that the use of alcohol is permitted only when it constitutes part of a medical treatment which is implemented "under the advice of a competent and conscientious physician, who may have to prescribe it for the cure of some special ailment".

(Baha'u'llah, The Kitab-i-Aqdas, p. 226)

278

Let those who seek good for themselves and others take note.[55] (Author's note-the rest of this chapter comes from the Wiki How website except as indicated.)

Know that the majority of rapes are committed by a person the victim knows. The statistics vary, but it is said that only 9%-33% of rapists were complete strangers to the victim.[3][4] This means that the vast majority of women are raped by men that they know, whether they are friends, people they are dating, co-workers, acquaintances, or even family members. This means that it's far more likely for a person to get raped by someone he/she knows instead of a stranger in a dark alley. Therefore, while it's important to take precautions when you're alone, you shouldn't completely let your guard down when you're with people you know.

- When you're in a social situation with someone you know, be extra careful and don't fully let your guard down unless you feel truly safe with the person. Even then, rape can occur. Know that if your gut tells you the situation is not okay, you should leave as soon and as safely as you can.
- Date rape is also extremely common -- according to one study, nearly 1/3 of rapes are committed by a date.[5] When you're dating someone new, understand that no absolutely means no, and don't ever let anyone make you feel guilty about knowing what you do and don't want. Don't be afraid to

---

[55] Author's notes that clarify the commandments of Baha'u'llah on alcohol and the notes from the Baha'i World Center in Haifa, Israel, in the Kitab-i-Aqdas: Baha'u'llah's Most Holy Book.

communicate your needs clearly and loudly, if necessary

Be aware of your surroundings at all times. Parking lots and parking garages are two of the sites that are most often targeted by attempted rapists. These people are predators, so view your surroundings carefully. If you are in a parking lot and feel someone is following you, start making noise -- talk to yourself loudly, talk to an imaginary person, or pretend to talk on your cell phone. The louder the potential victim, the more the predator is apt to freeze.[6]

• Scope out your surroundings during the day. Whether you're working in a new place or new to campus, make sure you learn the safest way to walk from place to place. This means staying under well-lit lights, walking in places where people tend to be around, and even being near blue light emergency call boxes, if your campus has them.

If you're in college, know that the majority of rapes happen during the first few weeks of the year. According to the Department of Justice, the majority of rapes in college occur during the first few weeks of your freshman and sophomore years.[7] These are the riskiest days because people are just getting to know each other, there are a lot of new people around, along with an abundance of alcohol. Though this shouldn't keep you from having fun or leaving your dorm room, you should be extra cautious about meeting new people, and make sure that you stick with your friends and your sound judgment.

Don't leave your drink unattended. Treat your drink like a $100.00 bill. Don't let anyone hold your drink. Avoid anything that somebody gives you. It could be "counterfeited." Always hold, keep and get your own drinks. Keep your hand over the top of your drink because it's easy to drop something into it. Do not accept a drink from a date unless the bartender or wait staff delivers it straight to you. Even if you're pretty sure the drink you left on the other side of the room was your drink, it's a much safer bet to buy or get another one.

Drink responsibly. Again, this does not mean that drinking irresponsibly makes it your fault if a rapist approaches you; it does, however, make you more vulnerable and susceptible to unwelcome attacks. Make sure not to drink more than 1 drink per hour (which means a glass of wine, a beer, or one shot of alcohol) and to stay in control of your mind and body as much as you can. Do *not* opt for the sketchy punch or jungle juice in a frat house; do not let anyone who is not a bartender make you a mixed drink because it is likely to be very, very strong.

Stick with your friends. Wherever you go, show up with a group of friends and leave with that group of friends. Even if you and your friends have ended up at different parts of the party, always know where your friends are and make sure that they see where you are, too. Keep in touch with your friends, make eye contact, and make sure you're on the same page. Your friends should have your back if they see you with a person whose company you don't want, and you should do the same. Don't leave your friend out with a person he/she's met for the first time, either, especially if there has been alcohol involved.

Be assertive. If somebody is giving you unwanted attention, tell them to back off. There is no need to be polite when somebody is making unwanted sexual advances. Firmly tell the person thanks, but no thanks, you're not interested. This may be more difficult if it's someone you actually know and care about, but it will still be possible. Once you get the message across, the person will be much more likely to move on.

Keep personal information private. Don't advertise your info verbally or on the Internet. Also, be very wary of meeting up with anyone whom you meet on the Internet. There is never a good reason to meet up with a person whom you have never met in person, or who talks you into meeting-up when you are hesitant. If you think you must do so, bring someone else, preferably a friend who is older and meet the person in a public place.

Always keep your phone charged. Don't step out with an almost-dead phone. It can be your saving grace, whether you need to call the cops or call your friends and ask them for help. Make sure you do this before you step out for the night, whether you're alone or with friends. You can even make a habit of bringing a charger out with you if you tend to forget it."[56]

How to Tell Someone "NO!"

When you find yourself in a situation with someone who is attempting to pressurize you into doing something you do not want to do, just say *No*. Do not concern yourself about hurting their feelings or that they won't want to see you again. In this kind of situation, worry only about your own feelings and thoughts. Do not ever allow yourself to be "talked" into doing anything that you do not want to do!

Shout *NO!* loudly and with conviction. That should surprise the perpetrator enough to stop the current situation and give you time to explain or put distance between you.

- If you find you are engaged in a serious physical struggle and you fear that you will be injured seriously or raped, as odd as it seems, there are some over-the-top things you can try, which certainly couldn't hurt: try acting crazy (shouting weird, nonsensical phrases, foaming at the mouth or drooling), throwing up if you can, peeing your pants, etc. It sounds bizarre, but if you can do something disgusting, it may shut down the physical struggle

---

[56] http://www.wikihow.com/Prevent-a-Potential-Rape

and give you time to escape. All's fair in situations like this.

- For females, in romantic situations where there is no response to your loud and emphatic NO, and you can't walk away, use the open palm of your hand to hit the offender in the nose with an upward motion. Do not use a fist - an open hand is more effective. Regardless of what Hollywood would have you think, this will not kill him. It will give him a bloody (and possibly broken) nose. For males, do not resort to violence unless it is absolutely necessary or the perpetrator is stronger than you.

- Remember that even though men generally don't strike women, bad things have happened when a man feels you have "led him on" and then denied him something. He may feel humiliated and angry, and may become aggressive. Aggressive outbursts in these situations have occurred involving even extremely low-key and mellow men. If you have had to resort to physical force in order to stop a man from touching you when you have asked him to stop, it is a dangerous situation. It shows that he was already prepared to use force to get his way, and the pain may fuel his anger considerably.

- Always follow through with your convictions. If you say *no*, then the answer is *no*, and must remain *no* until something changes.

- While it is taught that a man does not strike a woman, in certain dangerous situations, a man might be the one who is being assaulted and attacked. In a situation such as this, the man might have to use any means available to protect himself when saying 'no' is not enough.

- When you say *No* you have to mean it. Make sure that your verbal signals are clear and precise. Some think that saying "no" with a smile means something other than a clear "no".[57]

---

[57] http://www.wikihow.com/Tell-Someone-%22NO!%22

Appendix I

The <u>Cyrus the Great</u> Cylinder is the first charter of right of nations in the world. It is a baked-clay ritanni in Akkadian with cuneiform script. . This cylinder was excavated in 1879 by the Assyro-British archaeologist Hormuzd Rassam, foundations of the *Esagila* (the Marduk temple of Babylon) and is kept today in the British Museum in London.

On October 12 (Julian calendar; October 7 by the Gregorian calendar) 539 BC, Achaemanid army without any conflict entered the city of Babylon. Cyrus the Great himself, on October 29, entered the city, assuming the titles of *"king of Babylon, king of Sumer and Akkad, king of the four corners of the world"*. Cyrus The Great, on this cylinder, describes how he conquers the old city of Babylon and how his mighty army in peace marched into the city; his claim that he entered the city peacefully supports the same statement in the Chronicle of Nabonidus. The last king of Babylon, Nabonidus, is considered a tyrant with odd religious ideas, which causes Marduk, patron deity of the city of Babylon to intervene. Cyrus considers himself chosen by a supreme god, is confirmed by Second Isaiah, the chapters 40-55 of the Biblical book of Isaiah. The Cyrus Cylinder then was placed under the walls of *"Esagila"* as a foundation deposit, following a Mesopotamian tradition.

There were three main premises in the decrees of the Cyrus Cylinder: the political formulization of racial, linguistic, and religious equality, slaves and all deported peoples were to be allowed to return to home; and all destroyed temples were to be restored.[1]

In 1971, the Cyrus Cylinder was described as the world's first charter of human rights,[1, 2, 3, 4] and it was translated into all six official U.N. languages.[4] A replica of the cylinder is kept at the United Nations Headquarters in New York City in the second floor hallway, between the Security Council and the Economic and Social Council chambers.[5]

Passages in the text of cylinder have been interpreted as expressing Cyrus' respect for humanity, and as promoting a form of religious tolerance and freedom; and as result of his generous and humane policies, Cyrus gained the overwhelming support of his subjects.[6]

The Cyrus Cylinder is not the only reason that the Cyrus legacy is admired. According to Professor Richard Frye[7]:

"In short, the figure of Cyrus has survived throughout history as more than a great man who founded an empire. He became the epitome of the great qualities expected of a ruler in antiquity, and he assumed heroic features as a conqueror who was tolerant and magnanimous as well as brave and daring. His personality as seen by the Greeks influenced them and Alexander the Great, and, as the tradition was transmitted by the Romans, may be considered to influence our thinking even now."

Appendix II

Women's rights [edit]

The Declaration recognized many rights as belonging to citizens (who could only be male). This was despite the fact that after The March on Versailles on 5 October 1789, women presented the Women's Petition to the National Assembly in which they proposed a decree giving women equality.[*citation needed*] In 1790 Nicolas de Condorcet and Etta Palm d'Aelders unsuccessfully called on the National Assembly to extend civil and political rights to women.[22] Condorcet declared that "and he who votes against the right of another, whatever the religion, color, or sex of that other, has henceforth abjured his own".[23] The French Revolution did not lead to a recognition of women's rights and this prompted Olympe de Gouges to publish the Declaration of the Rights of Woman and the Female Citizen in September 1791.[24]

The Declaration of the Rights of Woman and the Female Citizen is modelled on the Declaration of the Rights of Man and of the Citizen and is ironic in formulation and exposes the failure of the French Revolution, which had been devoted to equality. It states that:

"This revolution will only take effect when all women become fully aware of their deplorable condition, and of the rights they have lost in society".

The *Declaration of the Rights of Woman and the Female Citizen* follows the seventeen articles of the *Declaration of the Rights of Man and of the Citizen* point for point and has been described by Camille Naish as "almost a parody... of the original document". The first article of the *Declaration of the Rights of Man and of the Citizen* proclaims that:

"Men are born and remain free and equal in rights. Social distinctions may be based only on common utility."

The first article of *Declaration of the Rights of Woman and the Female Citizen* replied:

"Woman is born free and remains equal to man in rights. Social distinctions may only be based on common utility".

De Gouges also draws attention to the fact that under French law women were fully punishable, yet denied equal rights, declaring "Women have the right to mount the scaffold, they must also have the right to mount the speaker's rostrum".[25]

Appendix III

Seneca Falls Convention
Elizabeth Cady Stanton and Lucritia Mott
July 1848
Declaration of Sentiments

When, in the course of human events, it becomes necessary for one portion of the family of man to assume among the people of the earth a position different from that which they have hitherto occupied, but one to which the laws of nature and of nature's God entitle them, a decent respect to the opinions of mankind requires that they should declare the causes that impel them to such a course.

We hold these truths to be self-evident: that all men and women are created equal; that they are endowed by their Creator with certain inalienable rights; that among these are life, liberty, and the pursuit of happiness; that to secure these rights governments are instituted, deriving their just powers from the consent of the governed. Whenever any form of government becomes destructive of these ends, it is the right of those who suffer from it to refuse allegiance to it, and to insist upon the institution of a new government, laying its foundation on such principles, and organizing its powers in such form, as to them shall seem most likely to effect their safety and happiness. Prudence, indeed, will dictate that governments long established should not be changed for light and transient causes; and accordingly all experience hath shown that mankind are more disposed to suffer, while evils are sufferable, than to right themselves by abolishing the forms to which they were accustomed. But when a long train of abuses and usurpations, pursuing invariably the same object, evinces a design to reduce them under absolute despotism, it is their duty to throw off such government, and to provide new guards for their future security. Such has been the patient sufferance of the women under this government, and such is now the necessity which constrains them to demand the equal station to which they are entitled.

The history of mankind is a history of repeated injuries and usurpations on the part of man toward woman, having in direct object the establishment of an absolute tyranny over her. To prove this, let facts be submitted to a candid world.

He has never permitted her to exercise her inalienable right to the elective franchise.

He has compelled her to submit to laws, in the formation of which she had no voice.

He has withheld from her rights which are given to the most ignorant and degraded men--both natives and foreigners.

Having deprived her of this first right of a citizen, the elective franchise, thereby leaving her without representation in the halls of legislation, he has oppressed her on all sides.

He has made her, if married, in the eye of the law, civilly dead.

He has taken from her all right in property, even to the wages she earns.

He has made her, morally, an irresponsible being, as she can commit many crimes with impunity, provided they be done in the presence of her husband. In the covenant of marriage, she is compelled to promise obedience to her husband, he becoming to all intents and purposes, her master-- the law giving him power to deprive her of her liberty, and to administer chastisement.

He has so framed the laws of divorce, as to what shall be the proper causes, and in case of separation, to whom the guardianship of the children shall be given, as to be wholly regardless of the happiness of women--the law, in all cases, going upon a false supposition of the supremacy of man, and giving all power into his hands.

After depriving her of all rights as a married woman, if single, and the owner of property, he has taxed her to support a government which recognizes her only when her property can be made profitable to it.

He has monopolized nearly all the profitable employments, and from those she is permitted to follow, she receives but a scanty remuneration. He closes against her all the avenues to wealth and distinction which he considers most honorable to himself. As a teacher of theology, medicine, or law, she is not known.

He has denied her the facilities for obtaining a thorough education, all colleges being closed against her.

He allows her in Church, as well as State, but a subordinate position, claiming Apostolic authority for her exclusion from the ministry, and, with some exceptions, from any public participation in the affairs of the Church.

He has created a false public sentiment by giving to the world a different code of morals for men and women, by which moral delinquencies which exclude women from society, are not only tolerated, but deemed of little account in man.

He has usurped the prerogative of Jehovah himself, claiming it as his right to assign for her a sphere of action, when that belongs to her conscience and to her God.

He has endeavored, in every way that he could, to destroy her confidence in her own powers, to lessen her self-respect, and to make her willing to lead a dependent and abject life.

Now, in view of this entire disfranchisement of one-half the people of this country, their social and religious degradation--in view of the unjust laws above mentioned, and because women do feel themselves aggrieved, oppressed, and fraudulently deprived of their most sacred rights, we insist that they have immediate admission to all the rights and privileges which belong to them as citizens of the United States.

In entering upon the great work before us, we anticipate no small amount of misconception, misrepresentation, and ridicule; but we shall use every instrumentality within our power to effect our object. We shall employ agents, circulate tracts, petition the State and National legislatures, and endeavor to enlist the pulpit and the press in our behalf. We hope this Convention will be followed by a series of Conventions embracing every part of the country.

Source: E.C. Stanton, S.B. Anthony and M.J. Gage, eds., *History of Woman Suffrage*, vol. 1 (1887), 70.

Appendix IV

UNIVERSAL DECLARATION
OF HUMAN RIGHTS[58]

PREAMBLE

Whereas recognition of the inherent dignity and of the equal and inalienable rights of all members of the human family is the foundation of freedom, justice and peace in the world,

Whereas disregard and contempt for human rights have resulted in barbarous acts which have outraged the conscience of mankind, and the advent of a world in which human beings shall enjoy freedom of speech and belief and freedom from fear and want has been proclaimed as the highest aspiration of the common people,

Whereas it is essential, if man is not to be compelled to have recourse, as a last resort, to rebellion against tyranny and oppression, that human rights should be protected by the rule of law,

Whereas it is essential to promote the development of friendly relations between nations,

---

[58] The Universal Declaration of Human Rights, which was adopted by the UN General Assembly on 10 December 1948, was the result of the experience of the Second World War.

Whereas the peoples of the United Nations have in the Charter reaffirmed their faith in fundamental human rights, in the dignity and worth of the human person and in the equal rights of men and women and have determined to promote social progress and better standards of life in larger freedom,

Whereas Member States have pledged themselves to achieve, in co-operation with the United Nations, the promotion of universal respect for and observance of human rights and fundamental freedoms,

Whereas a common understanding of these rights and freedoms is of the greatest importance for the full realization of this pledge,

Now, Therefore THE GENERAL ASSEMBLY proclaims THIS UNIVERSAL DECLARATION OF HUMAN RIGHTSas a common standard of achievement for all peoples and all nations, to the end that every individual and every organ of society, keeping this Declaration constantly in mind, shall strive by teaching and education to promote respect for these rights and freedoms and by progressive measures, national and international, to secure their universal and effective recognition and observance, both among the peoples of Member States themselves and among the peoples of territories under their jurisdiction.

Article 1.

- All human beings are born free and equal in dignity and rights.They are endowed with reason and conscience and should act towards one another in a spirit of brotherhood.

Article 2.

- Everyone is entitled to all the rights and freedoms set forth in this Declaration, without distinction of any kind, such as race, colour, sex, language, religion, political or other opinion, national or social origin, property, birth or other status. Furthermore, no distinction shall be made on the basis of the political, jurisdictional or international status of the country or territory to which a person belongs, whether it be independent, trust, non-self-governing or under any other limitation of sovereignty.

Article 3.

- Everyone has the right to life, liberty and security of person.

Article 4.

- No one shall be held in slavery or servitude; slavery and the slave trade shall be prohibited in all their forms.

Article 5.

- No one shall be subjected to torture or to cruel, inhuman or degrading treatment or punishment.

Article 6.

- Everyone has the right to recognition everywhere as a person before the law.

Article 7.

- All are equal before the law and are entitled without any discrimination to equal protection of the law. All are entitled to equal protection against any discrimination in violation of this Declaration and against any incitement to such discrimination.

Article 8.

- Everyone has the right to an effective remedy by the competent national tribunals for acts violating the fundamental rights granted him by the constitution or by law.

Article 9.

- No one shall be subjected to arbitrary arrest, detention or exile.

Article 10.

- Everyone is entitled in full equality to a fair and public hearing by an independent and impartial tribunal, in the determination of his rights and obligations and of any criminal charge against him.

Article 11.

- (1) Everyone charged with a penal offence has the right to be presumed innocent until proved guilty according to law in a public trial at which he has had all the guarantees necessary for his defence.
- (2) No one shall be held guilty of any penal offence on account of any act or omission which did not constitute a penal offence, under national or international law, at the time when it was committed. Nor shall a heavier penalty be imposed than the one that was applicable at the time the penal offence was committed.

Article 12.

- No one shall be subjected to arbitrary interference with his privacy, family, home or correspondence, nor to attacks upon his honour and reputation. Everyone has the right to the protection of the law against such interference or attacks.

Article 13.

- (1) Everyone has the right to freedom of movement and residence within the borders of each state.
- (2) Everyone has the right to leave any country, including his own, and to return to his country.

Article 14.

- (1) Everyone has the right to seek and to enjoy in other countries asylum from persecution.
- (2) This right may not be invoked in the case of prosecutions genuinely arising from non-political crimes or from acts contrary to the purposes and principles of the United Nations.

Article 15.

- (1) Everyone has the right to a nationality.
- (2) No one shall be arbitrarily deprived of his nationality nor denied the right to change his nationality.

Article 16.

- (1) Men and women of full age, without any limitation due to race, nationality or religion, have the right to marry and to found a family. They are entitled to equal rights as to marriage, during marriage and at its dissolution.

- (2) Marriage shall be entered into only with the free and full consent of the intending spouses.
- (3) The family is the natural and fundamental group unit of society and is entitled to protection by society and the State.

Article 17.

- (1) Everyone has the right to own property alone as well as in association with others.
- (2) No one shall be arbitrarily deprived of his property.

Article 18.

- Everyone has the right to freedom of thought, conscience and religion; this right includes freedom to change his religion or belief, and freedom, either alone or in community with others and in public or private, to manifest his religion or belief in teaching, practice, worship and observance.

Article 19.

- Everyone has the right to freedom of opinion and expression; this right includes freedom to hold opinions without interference and to seek, receive and impart information and ideas through any media and regardless of frontiers.

Article 20.

- (1) Everyone has the right to freedom of peaceful assembly and association.
- (2) No one may be compelled to belong to an association.

Article 21.

- (1) Everyone has the right to take part in the government of his country, directly or through freely chosen representatives.
- (2) Everyone has the right of equal access to public service in his country.
- (3) The will of the people shall be the basis of the authority of government; this will shall be expressed in periodic and genuine elections which shall be by universal and equal suffrage and shall be held by secret vote or by equivalent free voting procedures.

Article 22.

- Everyone, as a member of society, has the right to social security and is entitled to realization, through national effort and international co-operation and in accordance with the organization and resources of each State, of the economic, social and cultural rights indispensable for his dignity and the free development of his personality.

Article 23.

- (1) Everyone has the right to work, to free choice of employment, to just and favourable conditions of work and to protection against unemployment.
- (2) Everyone, without any discrimination, has the right to equal pay for equal work.
- (3) Everyone who works has the right to just and favourable remuneration ensuring for himself and his family an existence worthy of human dignity, and supplemented, if necessary, by other means of social protection.
- (4) Everyone has the right to form and to join trade unions for the protection of his interests.

Article 24.

- Everyone has the right to rest and leisure, including reasonable limitation of working hours and periodic holidays with pay.

Article 25.

- (1) Everyone has the right to a standard of living adequate for the health and well-being of himself and of his family, including food, clothing, housing and medical care and necessary social services, and the right to security in the event of unemployment, sickness, disability, widowhood, old age or other lack of livelihood in circumstances beyond his control.
- (2) Motherhood and childhood are entitled to special care and assistance. All children, whether

born in or out of wedlock, shall enjoy the same social protection.

Article 26.

- (1) Everyone has the right to education. Education shall be free, at least in the elementary and fundamental stages. Elementary education shall be compulsory. Technical and professional education shall be made generally available and higher education shall be equally accessible to all on the basis of merit.
- (2) Education shall be directed to the full development of the human personality and to the strengthening of respect for human rights and fundamental freedoms. It shall promote understanding, tolerance and friendship among all nations, racial or religious groups, and shall further the activities of the United Nations for the maintenance of peace.
- (3) Parents have a prior right to choose the kind of education that shall be given to their children.

Article 27.

- (1) Everyone has the right freely to participate in the cultural life of the community, to enjoy the arts and to share in scientific advancement and its benefits.
- (2) Everyone has the right to the protection of the moral and material interests resulting from any scientific, literary or artistic production of which he is the author.

Article 28.

- Everyone is entitled to a social and international order in which the rights and freedoms set forth in this Declaration can be fully realized.

Article 29.

- (1) Everyone has duties to the community in which alone the free and full development of his personality is possible.
- (2) In the exercise of his rights and freedoms, everyone shall be subject only to such limitations as are determined by law solely for the purpose of securing due recognition and respect for the rights and freedoms of others and of meeting the just requirements of morality, public order and the general welfare in a democratic society.
- (3) These rights and freedoms may in no case be exercised contrary to the purposes and principles of the United Nations.

Article 30.

- Nothing in this Declaration may be interpreted as implying for any State, group or person any right to engage in any activity or to perform any act aimed at the destruction of any of the rights and freedoms set forth herein.

Appendix V

Declaration of the Rights of Children

1. All children have the right to what follows, no matter what their race, color, sex, language, religion, political or other opinion, or where they were born or who they were born to.

2. You have the special right to grow up and to develop physically and spiritually in a healthy and normal way, free and with dignity.

3. You have a right to a name and to be a member of a country.

4. You have a right to special care and protection and to good food, housing and medical services.
5. You have a right to special care if handicapped in any way.

6. You have a right to love and understanding, preferably from parents and a family, but from the government where these cannot help.

7. You have a right to go to school for free, to play, and to have an equal chance to develop

yourself and to learn to be responsible and useful.

8. You have the right always to be among the first to get help.

9. You have the right to be protected against cruel acts or exploitation, e.g. you shall not be obliged to do work which hinders your development both physically and mentally.

You should not work before a minimum age and never when that would hinder your health and your moral and physical development.

10. You should be taught peace, understanding, tolerance, and friendship among all people.

Appendix VI

The International Day of the Girl Child

Theme for 2012: Ending Child marriage

On December 19, 2011, the United Nations General Assembly adopted <u>Resolution 66/170</u> to declare October 11 as the International Day of the Girl

Child, to recognize girls' rights and the unique challenges girls face around the world.

For its first observance, this year's Day will focus on child marriage, which is a fundamental human rights violation and impacts all aspects of a girl's life. Child marriage denies a girl of her childhood, disrupts her education, limits her opportunities, increases her risk to be a victim of violence and abuse, jeopardizes her health and therefore constitutes an obstacle to the achievement of nearly every Millennium Development Goal (MDG) and the development of healthy communities.

Globally, around one in three young women aged 20-24 years were first married before they reached age 18. One third of them entered into marriage before they turned 15. Child marriage results in early and unwanted pregnancies, posing life-threatening risks for girls. In developing countries, 90 per cent of births to adolescents aged 15-19 are to married girls, and pregnancy-related complications are the leading cause of death for girls in this age group.

Girls with low levels of schooling are more likely to be married early, and child marriage has been shown to virtually end a girl's education. Conversely, girls with secondary schooling are up to six times less likely to marry as children, making education one of the best strategies for protecting girls and combating child marriage.

Preventing child marriage will protect girls' rights and help reduce their risks of violence, early pregnancy, HIV infection, and maternal death and disability, including obstetric fistula. When girls are able to stay in school and avoid being married early, they can build a foundation for a better life for themselves and their families and participate in the progress of their nations.

Activities **and** events to mark the Day are organized by UNFPA, UNICEF, UN Women.

Governments in partnership with civil society actors and the international community are called upon to take urgent action to end the harmful practice of child marriage and to:

- Enact and enforce appropriate legislation to increase the minimum age of marriage for girls to 18 and raise public awareness about child marriage as a violation of girls' human rights.
- Improve access to good quality primary and secondary education, ensuring that gender gaps in schooling are eliminated.
- Mobilize girls, boys, parents, leaders, and champions to change harmful social norms, promote girls' rights and create opportunities for them.
- Support girls who are already married by providing them with options for schooling, sexual and reproductive health services,

livelihoods skills, opportunity, and recourse from violence in the home.

- Address the root causes underlying child marriage, including gender discrimination, low value of girls, poverty, or religious and cultural justifications.[59]

Appendix VII

Violence Against Women and Children

by The <u>Universal House of Justice</u>

Letter written 24 January 1993
published in *American Bahá'í*, pages 10-11 1993-11-23

Further to our letter of 14 November 1991, the Universal House of Justice has now completed its consideration of your letter of 21 September 1991, in which you raised a number of questions pertaining to violence and to the sexual abuse of women and

---

[59] http://www.un.org/en/events/girlchild/

children. We have been instructed to provide the following response to your questions.

As you know, the principle of the oneness of mankind is described in the Bahá'í Writings as the pivot round which all the Teachings of Bahá'u'lláh revolve. It has widespread implications which affect and remold all dimensions of human activity. It calls for a fundamental change in the manner in which people relate to each other, and the eradication of those age-old practices which deny the intrinsic human right of every individual to be treated with consideration and respect.

Within the family setting, the rights of all members must be respected. 'Abdu'l-Bahá has stated:

The integrity of the family bond must be constantly considered and the right of the individual members must not be transgressed. The rights of the son, the father, the mother - none of them must be transgressed, none of them must be arbitrary. Just as the son has certain obligations to his father, the father, likewise has certain obligations to his son. The mother, the sister, and other members of the household have their certain prerogatives. All these rights and prerogatives must be conserved...

The use of force by the physically strong against the weak, as a means of imposing one's will and fulfilling one's desires, is a flagrant transgression of the Bahá'í Teachings. There can be no justification for anyone

311

compelling another, through the use of force or through the threat of violence, to do that to which the other person is not inclined. 'Abdu'l-Bahá has written, "O ye lovers of God! In this, the cycle of Almighty God, violence and force, constraint and oppression, are one and all condemned." Let those who, driven by their passions or by their inability to exercise discipline in the control of their anger, might be tempted to inflict violence on another human being, be mindful of the condemnation of such disgraceful behaviour by the Revelation of Bahá'u'lláh.

Among the signs of moral downfall in the declining moral order are the high incidence of violence within the family, the increase of degrading and cruel treatment of spouses and children, and the spread of sexual abuse. It is essential that the members of the community of the Greatest Name take the utmost care not to be drawn into acceptance of such practices because of their prevalence. They must be ever mindful of their obligations to exemplify a new way of life distinguished by its respect for the dignity and rights of all people, by its exalted moral tone, and by its freedom from oppression and from all forms of abuse.

Consultation has been ordained by Bahá'u'lláh as the means by which agreement is to be reached and a collective course of action defined. It is applicable to the marriage partners and within the family, and indeed in all areas where believers participate in mutual decision-making. It requires all participants to express their opinions with absolute freedom and without apprehension that they will be censured and/or their views belittled; these prerequisites for success are unattainable if the fear of violence or abuse are present.

A number of your questions pertain to the treatment of women, and are best considered in light of the principle of equality of the sexes, which is set forth in the Bahá'í Teachings. This principle is far more than the enunciation of admirable ideals; it has profound implications in all aspects of human relations and must be an integral element of Bahá'í domestic and community life. The application of this principle gives rise to changes in habits and practices which have prevailed for many centuries. An example of this is found in the response provided on behalf of Shoghi Effendi to a question whether the traditional practices whereby the man proposes marriage to the woman is altered by the Bahá'í Teachings to permit the woman to issue a marriage proposal to the man; the response is, "The Guardian wishes to state that there is absolute equality between the two, and that no distinction of preference is permitted..." With the passage of time, during which Bahá'í men and women endeavour to apply more fully the principle of equality of the sexes, will come a deeper understanding of the far-reaching ramifications of this vital principle. As 'Abdu'l-Bahá has stated, "Until the reality of equality between men and women is established and attained, the highest social development of mankind is not possible."

The Universal House of Justice has in recent years urged that encouragement be given to Bahá'í women and girls to participate in greater measure in the social, spiritual and administrative activities of their communities, and has appealed to Bahá'í women to arise and demonstrate the importance of their role in all fields of service to the Faith.

For a man to use force to impose his will on a woman is a serious transgression of the Bahá'í Teachings. 'Abdu'l-Bahá has stated that:

The world in the past has been ruled by force, and man has dominated over woman by reason of his more forceful and aggressive qualities both of body and mind. But the balance is already shifting; force is losing its dominance, and mental alertness, intuition, and the spiritual qualities of love and service, in which woman is strong, are gaining ascendancy.

Bahá'í men have the opportunity to demonstrate to the world around them a new approach to the relationship between the sexes, where aggression and the use of force are eliminated and replaced by cooperation and consultation. The Universal House of Justice has pointed out in response to questions addressed to it that, in a marriage relationship, neither husband nor wife should ever unjustly dominate the other, and that there are times when the husband and the wife should defer to the wishes of the other, if agreement cannot be reached through consultation; each couple should determine exactly under what circumstances such deference is to take place.

From the pen of Bahá'u'lláh Himself has come the following statement on the subject of the treatment of women:

The friends of God must be adorned with the ornament of justice, equality, kindness and love. As they do not allow themselves to be the object of cruelty and transgression, in like manner they should not allow such tyranny to visit the handmaidens of God. He, verily, speaketh the truth and commandeth that which benefiteth His servants and handmaidens. He is the Protector of all in this world and the next.

No Bahá'í husband should ever beat his wife, or subject her to any form of cruel treatment; to do so would be an unacceptable abuse of the marriage relationship and contrary to the Teachings of Bahá'u'lláh.

The lack of spiritual values in society leads to a debasement of the attitudes which should govern the relationship between the sexes, with women being treated as no more that objects for sexual gratification and being denied the respect and courtesy to which all human beings are entitled. Bahá'u'lláh has warned: "They that follow their lusts and corrupt inclinations, have erred and dissipated their efforts. They, indeed, are of the lost." Believers might well ponder the exalted standard of conduct to which they are encouraged to aspire in the statement of Bahá'u'lláh concerning His "true follower", that: "And if he met the fairest and most comely of women, he would not feel his heart seduced by the least shadow of desire for her beauty. Such an one, indeed, is the creation of spotless chastity. Thus instructeth you the Pen of the Ancient of Days, as bidden by your Lord, the Almighty, the All-Bountiful."

One of the most heinous of sexual offences is the crime of rape. When a believer is a victim, she is entitled to the loving aid and support of the members of her community, and she is free to initiate action against the perpetrator under the law of the land should she wish to do so. If she become pregnant as a consequence of this assault, no pressure should be brought upon her to marry. As to whether she should continue or terminate the pregnancy, it is for her to decide on the course of action she should follow, taking into consideration medical and other relevant factors, and in the light of the Bahá'í Teachings. If she gives birth to a child as the result of rape, it is left to her discretion whether to seek financial support for the maintenance of the child from the father; however, his claim to any parental rights would, under Bahá'í law, be called into question, in view of the circumstances.

The Guardian has clarified, in letters written on his behalf that, "The Bahá'í Faith recognizes the value of the sex impulse," and that, "The proper use of the sex instinct is the natural right of every individual, and it is precisely for this very purpose that the institution of marriage has been established." In this aspect of the marital relationship, as in all others, mutual consideration and respect should apply. If a Bahá'í woman suffers abuse or is subjected to rape by her husband, she has the right to turn to the Spiritual Assembly for assistance and counsel, or to seek legal protection. Such abuse would gravely jeopardize the continuation of the marriage, and could well lead to a condition of irreconcilable antipathy.

You have raised several questions about the treatment of children. It is clear from the Bahá'í Writings that a vital component of the education of children is the exercise of discipline. Shoghi Effendi has stated, in a letter written on his behalf about the education of children, that:

Discipline of some sort, whether physical, moral, or intellectual is indeed indispensable, and no training can be said to be complete and fruitful if it disregards this element. The child when born is far from being perfect. It is not only helpless, but actually is imperfect, and even is naturally inclined toward evil. He should be trained, his natural inclinations harmonized, adjusted and controlled, and if necessary suppressed or regulated, so as to ensure his healthy physical and moral development. Bahá'í parents cannot simply adopt an attitude of non-resistance towards their children, particularly those who are unruly and violent by nature. It is not even sufficient that they should pray on their behalf. Rather they should endeavour to inculcate, gently and patiently, into their youthful minds such principles and teachings of the Cause with such tactful and loving care as would enable them to become "true sons of God" and develop into loyal and intelligent citizens of His Kingdom...

While the physical discipline of children is an acceptable part of their education and training, such actions are to be carried out "gently and patiently" and with "loving care", far removed from the anger and violence with which children are beaten and abused in some parts of the world. To treat children in such an abhorrent manner is a denial of their human rights, and a betrayal of the trust which the weak should have in the strong in a Bahá'í community.

It is difficult to imagine a more reprehensible perversion of human conduct that the sexual abuse of children, which finds its most debased form in incest. At a time in the fortunes of humanity when, in the words of the Guardian, "The perversion of human nature, the degradation of human conduct, the corruption and dissolution of human institutions, reveal themselves...in their worst and most revolting aspects, and when "the voice of human conscience is stilled", when "the sense of decency and shame is obscured," the Bahá'í institutions must be uncompromising and vigilant in their commitment to the protection of the children entrusted to their care, and must not allow either threats or appeals to expediency to divert them from their duty. A parent who is aware that the marriage partner is subjecting a child to such sexual abuse should not remain silent, but must take all necessary measures, with the assistance of the Spiritual Assembly or civil authorities if necessary, to bring about an immediate cessation of such grossly immoral behaviour, and to promote healing and therapy.

Bahá'u'lláh has placed great emphasis on the duties of parents toward their children, and He has urged children to have gratitude in their hearts for their parents, whose good pleasure they should strive to win as a means of pleasing God Himself. However, He has indicated that under certain circumstances, the parents could be deprived of their right to parenthood as a consequence of their actions. The Universal House of Justice has the right to legislate on this matter. It has decided for the present that all cases should be referred to it in which the conduct or character of a parent appears to render him unworthy of having such parental rights as that of giving consent to a marriage. Such questions could arise, for example, when a parent has committed incest, or when the child was conceived as the consequence of rape, and also when a parent consciously fails to protect the child from flagrant sexual abuse.

As humanity passes through the age of transition in its evolution to a world civilization which will be illumined by spiritual values and will be distinguished by its justice and its unity, the role of the Bahá'í community is clear: it must accomplish a spiritual transformation of its members, and must offer to the world a model of the society destined to come into being through the power of the Revelation of Bahá'u'lláh. Membership in the Bahá'í community is open to all who accept Bahá'u'lláh as the Manifestation of God, and who thereupon embark on the process of changing their conduct and refining their character. It is inevitable that this community will, at times, be subject to delinquent behaviour of members whose actions do not conform to the standards of the Teachings. At such times, the institutions of the Faith will not hesitate to apply Bahá'í law with justice and fairness in full confidence that this Divine Law is the means for the true happiness of all concerned. However, it should be recognized that the ultimate solution to the problems of humanity lies not in penalties and punishments, but rather in spiritual education and illumination. 'Abdu'l-Bahá has written:

It is incumbent upon human society to expend all its forces on the education of the people, and to copiously water men's hearts with the sacred steams that pour down from the realm of the All-Merciful, and to teach them the manners of heaven and spiritual ways of life, until every member of the community of man will be schooled, refined and exalted to such a degree of perfection that the very committing of a shameful act will seem in itself the direst infliction and most agonizing of punishments, and man will fly in terror and seek refuge in his God from the very idea of crime, as something far harsher and more grievous than the punishment assigned to it.

It is toward this goal that the community of the Greatest Name is striving, aided and reinforced by the limitless power of the Holy Spirit.

Appendix VIII

Towards the Eradication of Violence Against Women and Girls

http://www.bic.org/statements/towards-eradication-violence-against-women-and-girls

Baha'i International Community's contribution to the 57th Session of the Commission on the Status of Women

15 November 2012

New York

The epidemic of violence and discrimination against women and girls is once again on the global agenda. The efforts of governments, civil society organizations, and individuals at the local, national and international levels have led to the development of legal and institutional frameworks to protect the rights of women and girls and have called attention to the culture of impunity within which violence against women is often tolerated and even condoned.

Women and girls in territories throughout the world are enmeshed in a culture which enables and sustains violence against them. This affects not only women and girls; such violence is ultimately an act of aggression against society as a whole. It degrades victims, perpetrators, families and entire communities. As such, the eradication of violence requires not only changes in law and policy, but more fundamental changes at the level of culture, attitudes and beliefs. Such changes must be grounded in the conviction that the equality of women and men is not only a goal to be achieved, but a truth about human nature to be acknowledged and embraced. The soul has no gender. The very essence of what make us human is neither 'male' nor 'female.' Conceived in this way, equality goes beyond a tally of resources or a set of social norms. It reflects the nobility inherent in every human being.

Viewed in the broader context, violence and discrimination against women and girls is one of the symptoms of a social order characterized by conflict, injustice and insecurity. Its structures and processes—constrained by particularistic agendas— prove themselves incapable of serving the common good. As we seek to eradicate violence against women and girls, we must not lose sight of the broader, long-term goal: namely the creation of conditions in which women *and* men can work shoulder to shoulder in constructing a more just and equitable social order.

We offer the following recommendations for consideration by the Commission:

Prevailing conceptions of power and empowerment need to be redefined. The 2006 'In-depth study on all forms of violence against women' stated that "structural imbalances of power and inequality between women and men are both the context and causes of violence against women" (A/61/122/Add.1). Yet an improved balance of power will not suffice. The very conception of power needs to be seriously questioned and fundamentally redefined. Prevailing notions of power tend to focus on the ability to compete effectively, to dominate, and to gain ascendancy over others. These essentially adversarial expressions of power do not provide society with the tools needed to create institutions and processes that foster the progress of all members of the community. The dominant thinking of power as 'power over' must be replaced with the concept of 'power to'—power as a capacity of the individual or of the collective. We need a broadened appreciation of the sources of power available to humanity, such as power that comes from the bonds of solidarity and mutual concern, and power that emanates from unity of thought and action, and the promotion of such qualities as justice, honesty, and integrity.

The Commission has repeatedly noted that the empowerment of women and girls is key to protecting their human rights and breaking the cycle of violence. Empowerment is a process of recognition, capacity building and action. Individuals become empowered as they come to recognize their inherent worth, the fundamental equality of all human beings, and their ability to improve their own condition and that of the wider society. At the collective level, empowerment involves the transformation of relationships of dominance into relationships of equality and mutuality.

The role of men in addressing this violence and exploitation has been recognized as a key aspect of prevention. Men and boys must be encouraged to speak out strongly against violence and exploitation and not to protect perpetrators. They must make a conscious effort to understand fully the principle of the equality of women and men and its expression in both private and public life. At home, men must come to understand their role in modeling healthy relations and respect for male and female members of the family. It is often in the home that boys and girls first learn about the nature of power and how it is expressed. Distorted expressions of power and authority promote in children attitudes and habits that are carried to the workplace, to the community, and to public life.

The international community and the State must shift from reactive approaches to ones that focus on prevention of violence. Prevention must begin by identifying and addressing the underlying causes of the violence rather than its symptoms. Efforts aims at prevention must consider the prevailing conceptions of gender identity and of power, and the forms of discrimination and disadvantage that place women and girls at risk of violence. While States have initiated various prevention programs, these have been hampered by an overall lack of societal transformation. Such transformation involves changes at the level of attitudes, culture, community life, as well as in the structures that sustain and normalize violence and exploitation. To date, the majority of prevention activity has been carried out by civil society organizations, with limited resources. States need to assume greater responsibility for the implementation of policies and programmes that such transformation requires and support the initiatives of civil society. In addition, more research is needed to determine strategies to prevent violence against girls and women in States that are fragile or in the midst of conflict or post-conflict recovery.

One approach towards social transformation is through the education and training of children and youth in a manner that cultivates in them a sense of dignity as well as responsibility for the well-being of their family members and for the wider community. Drawing on the experiences of the worldwide Baha'i community in promoting social transformation, we note a number of elements in educational endeavors that support such transformation: a conviction that happiness and honor lie in integrity; the ability to act with moral courage; the ability to participate in non-adversarial decision-making; a degree of excellence in a productive skill through which one can meet one's needs with dignity; the ability to analyze social conditions and understand the forces that shape them; the ability to express ideas eloquently and wisely; the capacity to foster collaboration; and an emphasis on service to the community. While emphasis must continue to be placed on girls' access to quality education, due attention must be given to the education of boys particularly with respect to issues of gender equality.

No custom, tradition, or religious interpretation that sanctions any form of violence against women and girls should be allowed to outweigh the obligation to eradicate violence against women and girls. The regrettable practice of hiding behind cultural and religious traditions that permit violence against women perpetuates a climate of legal and moral impunity. The responsibility of States to protect women and girls from violence must take precedence over any such customs. Religious leaders, who play an instrumental role in shaping attitudes and beliefs, must also support unequivocally the principle of the equality of women and men. Practices and doctrines which condone or promote violence against women and girls need to be eliminated. It must also be remembered that all religions contain the voices of women. Too often, due to ignorance, lack of education or lack of opportunity to be heard, the views of women have been absent from the definition of what religion is and how its teachings bear on public and private life.

States must take comprehensive measures to eradicate the culture of impunity. The individual, her family and her community are under the protection of the State. Yet, a culture of impunity persists in many territories: perpetrators of violence against and exploitation of women and girls go unpunished (or inadequately punished). The victims of such acts have little or no means of redress and or access to support services. More needs to be done to prevent the violence and exploitation of women and girls. All too often, for example, inadequate resources are allocated to implement laws that protect women and specialized services for victims do not exist. In many cases of violence and abuse, the web of actors is extensive and the pressures to remain silent about the abuse are strong. Penalties for perpetrators must be accompanied by measures to ensure the security of victims, who often need protection from retribution. The incorporation of commitments made in Security Council resolutions related to women, peace and security, into national action plans has been a positive step in this regard.

[i] Bahá'u'lláh, HWA #51

[ii] The Báb, BP, Baha'i Publishing Trust, © 2002, p. 28

[iii] Hidden Words Persian #32

[iv] Hidden Words Arabic #40

[v] Daisies or candles could also be chosen

[vi] Gleanings from the Writings of Bahá'u'lláh, p. 259

[vii] This definition of authority of self, was created by the author, who also wrote Assisting the Traumatized Soul: Healing the Wounded Talisman.

[viii] Ian Semple, member of the Universal House of Justice, from an address titled "Obedience" presented in connection with the Spiritual Enrichment Program at the Bahá'í World Center, July 26, 1991.

[ix] N. Josefowitz, *Paths to Power,* p. 4.

[x] Secret of Divine Civilization, p. 1

[xi] Bahá'u'lláh, GL, p. 164-165

[xii] HWA #51

[xiii] Universal House of Justice, Compilation of Compilations, Vol. 1, p. 111

[xiv] BP, Tablet of Ahmad, p. 210

[xv] Gleanings, p. 149

[xvi] Shoghi Effendi, 28 October 1935

[xvii] PUP, p. 291

[xviii] Compilation of Compilations, p. 93

[xix] Tablets of Bahá'u'lláh, p. 35

[xx] Some Answered Questions, Baha'i Publishing Trust, © 1981, p. 210

[xxi] KA, ¶ 1

[xxii] GWB, p. 143

[xxiii] TB, p. 66

[xxiv] GWB, p. 262

[xxv] TB, p. 63

[xxvi] See also HWA #24 and HWP #43

[xxvii] 'Abdu'l-Bahá, PUP, p. 291

[xxviii] 'Abdu'l-Bahá, SAQ, p. 300

[xxix] TB, p. 72

[xxx] PUP, p. 49

[xxxi] Ps. 27:13-14

[xxxii] An Early Pilgrimage, p. 40

[xxxiii] Graduate Students in Iowa followed a two year old child around for a day and discovered that the ratio of "noes" to "yes's" was 13 to 1. The national average between parent and child is 12 to 1. And the teacher/student ratio in a secondary school classroom is 18 to 1. The date of this information is unknown. However this note came from Thomas F. Crum, *The Magic of Conflict*, Touchstone, Simon and Schuster, NY, 1988.

[xxxiv] Phyllis K. Peterson, "Healing the Wounded Soul."

www.ingramcontent.com/pod-product-compliance
Lightning Source LLC
Chambersburg PA
CBHW071638270326
41928CB00010B/1970